more praise f

Sister Reve

Sister Rebel is a rare account of how the inner life drives the outer one. Theresa Bonpane's story proves justice is love in action. Young Theresa Killeen worried that God's will for her meant surrendering ordinary life to vows of chastity, poverty, and obedience, following the submissive example Mother Mary offered to Catholic girls: "Be it done unto me according to Thy Word." But as a nun, Theresa slowly realized religious life wasn't authentic for her, so she took "the leap" that required tremendous courage from one taught it would only land in hellfire. In fact, she created communities of peace and justice with every new step, starting a halfway house for the ex-religious; teaching in LA schools; working among immigrants and the unhoused. When she married Blase Bonpane, a priest who'd left religious vows to commit more freely to organizing for peace and justice, they raised their children while working with the United Farm Workers, and, when they returned to LA, they endured death threats and official opprobrium to ignite a peace movement that has global reach. This book gives me hope for the future of the planet.
—**Mimi Kennedy**, actress, author, and activist

Theresa Bonpane's new book, *Sister Rebel*, is a must-read for anyone who's been involved in the peace & justice/anti-war movement. Her life has been such an incredible journey. Theresa was the codirector of the Office of the Americas for over twenty-five years with her late husband, Blase Bonpane. I worked with them for many years and always referred to them as the 'heart and soul' of the movement. Her story is one that most anyone will want to read, whether they are in the movement or not.
—**Frank Dorrel**, publisher of *Addicted to War: Why the U.S. Can't Kick Militarism* by Joel Andreas

Sister Rebel is a brutally honest view of life inside a convent and life inside a justice movement. Through her triumphs, struggles, and pain in these very different places, Theresa Bonpane never loses her agency or courage. She stays honest and focused on the cause despite the dramatic changes in her living conditions, her finances, her relationships, her roles, and her perceptions of the world. Ms. Bonpane shares the common and unfortunate phenomenon of an organization working for systemic change in the community while failing to create that equity within their own organization. She understands firsthand that there are times to stay and times to move on. *Sister Rebel* is a riveting book about a courageous, honest organizer who is not afraid of the unknown. Power struggles and personal attacks don't slow her down. She models how to tell the truth even to beloved leaders, and how to persist with what is right.

—**Rev. Janet McKeithen**, cofounder of the Committee for Racial Justice

Sister Rebel

A MEMOIR

Theresa Killeen Bonpane

XENO

Library of Congress Cataloging-in-Publication Data

Names: Bonpane, Theresa, 1935– author.
Title: Sister rebel: a memoir / Theresa Bonpane.
Description: Pasadena, CA: Xeno, [2023]
Identifiers: LCCN 2023002110 (print) | LCCN 2023002111 (ebook) | ISBN
  9781939096081 (paperback) | ISBN 9781939096142 (casebound) | ISBN
  9781939096111 (ebook)
Subjects: LCSH: Bonpane, Theresa, 1935– | Ex-nuns—United
  States—Biography. | Maryknoll Sisters—Biography. | Political
  activists—United States—Biography. | Pacifists—United
  States—Biography. | Office of the Americas—History.
Classification: LCC BX4668.3.B675 A3 2023 (print) | LCC BX4668.3.B675
  (ebook) | DDC 271/.9002 [B]—dc23/eng/20230428
LC record available at https://lccn.loc.gov/2023002110
LC ebook record available at https://lccn.loc.gov/2023002111

The National Endowment for the Arts, the Los Angeles County Arts Commission, the Los Angeles Department of Cultural Affairs, the City of Pasadena Cultural Affairs Division, Sony Pictures Entertainment, and the Dwight Stuart Youth Fund partially support Red Hen Press.

First Edition
XENO Books is an imprint of Red Hen Press, Pasadena, CA
www.redhen.org/xeno

Has any writer ever said, "This book would not exist except for the role of my publishers?" Perhaps not, but it is absolutely true in my case. Without the presence of Kate Gale and Mark Cull of Red Hen Press in my life, it would still be in my memory, my heart, but never in a book. Their encouragement, professionalism, hard work, and their friendship made it happen and I can't thank them enough.

This book is the result of my life.

I dedicate it to my husband, Blase Bonpane,
present for our fifty years of sharing life and love.

To my children and grandchildren
for their added beauty to our lives.
Colleen and John Londono and their children,
Blase Jairo, Chiara, and Gianna Londono.
Blase Martin and Jen and their children,
Ossian, Nola, and Blase Scott Briar Bonpane.

Also, to my parents, Winifred and Martin Killeen,
for their lifelong inspiration of lives lived in total kindness ,
simplicity, and profound spiritual values of love and generosity.

To *ALL* with whom I have shared the last eighty-eight years of my life
and who have helped me to live a life of challenges,
Love and joy.

ALLELUIA!

CONTENTS

Publisher's Note

This memoir has been compiled from interviews, recordings, letters, and personal notes from Theresa Bonpane's personal archive. Interviews conducted by Therese Barnett were at the behest of the University of California Los Angeles's Center for Oral History Research. Interviews conducted by Carol Laslanne were conducted at the Office of the Americas.

Sister Rebel

CHAPTER 1

A Troy, New York Childhood

I was born in Troy, New York, on March 14, 1935, the eighth child in my family.

Rumor has it that my mother, Winifred Killeen, delivered me at home while she was looking at a picture of St. Joseph. We didn't have a telephone, we didn't have a car, and I guess I just decided I was coming, so my father, Martin Killeen, had to run out to the grocery store or someplace to find a phone to call an ambulance. Meantime, I had already started arriving. My mother claimed that she just looked at St. Joseph and said, "It's all yours. It's up to you now."

Both of my parents were born in Ireland. They didn't know each other there, but when they arrived in the United States, like many Irish immigrants, they went to New York City for their new lives. They had no money. They'd both had just six years of education, which was fairly typical outside of the upper class. Only six years of education, coming to a new country, and they had to struggle, struggle, struggle all the time. My father tried to get a lot of different jobs, and, finally, he found one as a welder at the Ford Motor Company in Troy, New York. My mother, occasionally, in between those eight children, was a domestic worker.

We were quite poor, but I never heard an argument about money. To them, everything was God's will, and who were they to question that? They said, "God will provide," even though it often didn't seem like he was providing. Even paying rent on a regular basis was difficult. We were always struggling. We never had anything extra at all: we ate, we had a roof over our heads, and most of our clothes came from rummage sales, where the poorest of the poor went to rummage through other people's discarded clothes. That was just how we lived at that time.

Those were still the years of the Great Depression. My parents, like most poor people then, identified as Democrats, but they were basically apolitical. They did like Franklin D. Roosevelt—I mean, he worked for the poor, and he had those programs, so they thought he must be a good guy, plus he was a Democrat. Aside from that, we never discussed politics. We weren't readers, either. I don't think we ever had books in our house. We got a local paper that would tell about the local robberies, but that was pretty much all the political discussion we had in our home.

Troy was a very small town right next to Albany. We lived in South Troy, which was the wrong side of the tracks, in the immigrant neighborhood. Italians lived together in one part, the Irish in another part, the Germans in another, but they were all Catholics, and they all had their own churches. There was the German Catholic Church, the French Catholic Church, the Irish Catholic Church, and the Italian Catholic Church. We all came together in school, but we were pretty isolated from any other ethnic groups outside of that.

I hate to say it, but in retrospect, my father had a little bit of Archie Bunker in him. Not the meanness, but the idea that the Irish should stick with their own; your own are the best; the Irish are the best, and don't mix up with any of the others in terms of dating or getting married. Most of all, my father warned us to stay away from the Italians, because they had no morals. Of course, my husband, Blase, is Italian.

My father, like most of the Irish at that time, was totally under the thumb of the Catholic Church. Totally. Whatever the bishop or priest said to do, that's what we did. In terms of making sure the commandments of the church were followed, my father was almost holier than the pope: we all went to Mass every Sunday, we went to communion, and we went to confession. We were strict Catholics, very obedient to everything. I often think that it was like a part of our brains were frozen; there were things we simply never thought to question. If the priest or someone said something irrational, we never said, "Hmmm, that doesn't really make any sense." If the priest said it, that was all we needed to know. This was entirely contrary to the way my husband, Blase, was brought up. He and his father questioned everything.

Almost from the day I was born, I was taught that God had created me, and the purpose of my life—or any person's life, for that matter—was to give it over to God. His will be done. Of course, as far as knowing what His will was, that was a completely different matter. This certainly wasn't a bad way to grow up—far from it. I was given a strong sense that there was something far more important than the material world and day-to-day existence.

Our Catholic upbringing emphasized that we were here on this earth for one reason alone: to serve God, and do whatever God asked us to do. The cornerstone of our teachings was sacrifice. No matter what God asked of you, no matter how hard it was, that was what you should do. That was the essential key to why I eventually entered a convent.

My Catholic education set impossible goals, and this inevitably led to guilt. In my family, there was no such thing as the idea that being good makes you feel good, or that trying to do the right thing was enough. There was just pure blind duty. The catechism said: "do this," or "don't do that," and you simply accepted it as a matter of fact. No questions asked. Any deviation from the catechism translated into sin. Which created guilt. Which led to despair. Which meant going to hell. This meant that you had to go to confession, as this was your only hope for redemption.

My mother was a very sweet, very kind person. She didn't have a mean bone in her body, but she definitely was not on the job with me as a mother. I don't have any remembrance of her mothering me; you know, "Let me do your hair," or anything like that. I thought being the eighth child had something to do with this, and my older sisters were around to help with that kind of thing, and my father was absolutely adoring.

I found out many, many years later, when I was about forty years old, that my mother had had a nervous breakdown right after I was born. Her seventh child was born a little more than a year before me and died just two months later. She had just carried and lost a baby, and then immediately fell pregnant with me. I'm sure she was still mourning the loss of her seventh child throughout her pregnancy. And then she had yet another child to care for.

My father was really both mother and father to me. My relationship with my mother was cordial, and we got along, but it was not much of a mother-daughter relationship.

Theresa's father and uncles, 1920.

I remember making the conscious realization that my mother was not going to push me or help me in any way, that I was basically looking out for myself. I was in the first grade, and I had woken up too late to go to school. I said to my mother, "Look what time it is! I'm late for school." Winters in upstate New York were freezing, and my mother just replied, "Oh, Theresa, it's too cold to go to school. It's fine."

That's when I first knew that I was sort of on my own. My mother didn't care whether I went to school or not, so it was up to me to make sure I went.

I was a bit of a goodie-goodie. My family had a reputation for being late, and I wanted to do everything exactly right. I had to be in school every day, and I always had to make sure I was there on time. I had to wake up early every morning to iron my uniform, because my mother certainly never helped me with anything like that. Our family's reputation was a little embarrassing to me—I didn't want to get in trouble, and I wanted to do the right thing.

I went to Catholic schools all my life. I don't remember a lot of details about elementary school, but I do remember second grade. My teacher that year, Sister Frances, is one of the few nuns that I still remember from back then. She had a great influence on my life.

In catechism class with Sister Frances, there was one particular catechism that always stuck with me. There were three milk bottles: one was pure white, free of sin; one specked with black, representing the soul tarnished by committing venial sins; and one as black as coal, all of God's grace removed by committing mortal sins. The black bottle was the soul that would be sent to hell for all eternity. The white bottle was the soul able to enter the kingdom of Heaven. The one in between, the speckled bottle, would go to purgatory for fifty thousand years. They seemed to ask us which milk bottle we were going to choose to be. Where would our souls end up?

That image of the three milk bottles was implanted in my mind. In everything I did, I thought, "Now, let's see. This was a venial sin, this was a mortal sin . . ." Of course, the mortal sins were the really dangerous ones, because they were much harder to atone for and get rid of. This thought process of categorizing my every sin influenced my life very much. I spent a lot of time worrying about being a good person so I didn't end up in purgatory or hell. I remember looking at my mother, who was forty-nine years old at the time (which, at my age, seemed closer to one hundred and forty-nine), and thinking, "I'll never be able to be good for that long!"

Theresa in elementary school, 1947.

By the second grade, I had pretty much learned that being good all the time wasn't so easy. One day, the principal came into the room and asked, "May I see Theresa Killeen?" I didn't think anything of it—I was always being called to run errands or deliver messages. After all, I was a good kid from a respectable family. But as soon as I got outside, she started shaking the living daylights out of me. She said that Billy Gardner, one of our so-called friends, had spotted Suney Tata and me smoking! If my parents didn't already know about it, she was going to call them up and make sure they did. She asked me, didn't I know what a bad little child I was for hanging around Suney Tata? Well, I hadn't before, but I certainly knew then.

So by the time I was seven, I had a pretty clear indication of what the rest of my life was going to bring. On one hand, I was a good kid, a holy kid. On the other, a deviant, a sinner. And to make matters worse, I generally gave the impression of enjoying myself in both sides of my life, which would end up complicating things down the road.

Then came fourth grade and Sister Bernadine, a horror of a nun. She taught us that public schools and their students were bad, a sure-fire road to perdition, and were to be avoided at all costs. A main factor in this hatred of public schools was racism—she was disgusted by schools that admitted Black students, and she feared the students themselves and those who associated with them—which she tried to instill in us. Even at that age, I recall having a strong sense that what she was teaching was wrong and that she was behaving horribly as a nun. Didn't God create them as well?

Sixth grade was something of a turning point for me. It was when I met Danny Dwyer, my first "real" boyfriend. He came to my defense when Sister Florence accused me of cheating while she was out of the classroom. I really resented her for that—of course I hadn't cheated! I was serious about my schoolwork, and I was raised to be honest. I was so outraged that I actually raised my voice against her, something I almost never did. But Danny had defended me.

I was only eleven years old, but I was in love. Come seventh grade, we were in the same class and my crush was so overwhelming, it was beginning to manifest itself in increasingly poor marks. Eventually, Sister Elaine took me aside and told me I was boy crazy. I wasn't, though, I thought to myself. I just had a crush. She thought that because of that and because I hung around the boys sometimes, I had something other than education on my mind. But I was still a good girl—I said my prayers, attended the novenas, and I still went to First Friday Mass with my father.

High school was a completely new experience for me; except for being led by nuns and priests, it bore no resemblance to my grade school days. I was no longer confined to the environment of South Troy and was being exposed to a whole different group of people from various economic classes. This was exhilarating, but even high school had a ways of dividing us based on our backgrounds. Because we were from South Troy, no one ever asked, "Do you think you'll go to college, so you'll need to take algebra and you'll need to take this course and that course?" They just said, "Okay, secretarial practice, business law, trade school . . ." No one ever explained it, we never talked about it: they just told us what subjects we would be taking. None of us ever questioned it. We just took whatever courses they said we should.

Theresa (top left) with her family, 1951.

At that time, my only interest was my social life. I honestly only thought of school as a place to go to have fun. Up through sixth grade, I had been an honor student who'd made all A's. Starting in seventh grade, I began to drift a little. Maybe Sister Elaine had been right. I had a crush on this guy and a crush on that one, and then I was busy going out with my friends to the movies, or maybe to a dance or a party. I didn't have much time to focus on anything else, nor did I want to. From then on, it was all about my social life and meeting guys and going out and having a good time.

By high school, I was a serious smoker. No more puffing for me—I was even an inhaler. For me and my friends, the height of entertainment was hanging out, smoking, telling stories, and getting into a little mischief. Everything else was lost on us. And we more or less welcomed that lifestyle with open arms.

But really, we weren't bad. We were regular teenagers. Most of us earned our money babysitting, we went to Mass just like everyone else, and, like other people, we enjoyed hanging out and talking. But to the nuns, we were young women of questionable virtue. I was no longer in the old neighborhood, so none of them knew me or were aware that I came from a good, respectable family. Without question or pause, they were always sitting us down and giving us talks about minding our chastity and staying on the straight and narrow.

Some of my teachers, particularly my homeroom teacher, didn't like me much, especially because I was popular and was elected as the homeroom president. In addition to being from South Troy, of all places, I lacked seriousness and academic rigor, and I had started dating at a scandalously young age (if you consider freshman year scandalously young). To some of the nuns, this meant I didn't deserve my popularity.

When I was a freshman, we had a class called "Charm Personality Club," which was basically a morality course full of all kinds of bizarre rules and advice. Rules like, "a good Catholic schoolgirl should never kiss a boy until the third date." Nothing more than a little kiss, though—French kissing was, of course, a mortal sin. Even now, I can't tell if this class was meant to help us or scare us.

I got to go to all the proms, which meant I was pretty lucky. We didn't have a lot of money, so most of my gowns were borrowed and nearly all of them were strapless, which was strictly forbidden. My friends and I would wrap ourselves in shawls, but it didn't do much to disguise the fact that our shoulders were bare. Sister Frederica was there with the camera to verify it. To her, it was just one more indication that we were fast girls. That reputation followed me throughout high school.

To the nuns, there was something inherently wrong about a young girl from South Troy being as popular as I was, getting elected class president, and having an active social life. In their mind, the only way a person could earn such popularity was by doing something extra for it. This accusation was unfair and untrue. So I grew defensive. I felt I had something to prove to them. I was a better girl than they made me out to be, and I wanted to show them that being good and having a good time were not mutually exclusive.

Theresa (left) and friends enjoying prom, 1951.

During my sophomore year, I was elected homeroom president again and began dating the captain of the basketball team, a straight-A student and all-around respectable boy, much to the chagrin of the teacher. To her, he was a good, moral lad, and I was clearly out to corrupt him. She tried to stop us from seeing one another, saying I wasn't good enough for him. I'm still not sure what exactly it was about me that inspired such ire; all I know is that I received more than my fair share of the nuns' hostility.

Still, high school was a great place to socialize. I was a bridge between the rich and the poor: my girlfriends were from South Troy, but my boyfriends were from North Troy. The nuns resented me, and of course, those three milk bottles were always there in the back of my mind. So I started attending First Friday Mass again, which I felt made me just a little bit holier.

Theresa as a freshman at the beach, 1953.

Ditching school became a new hobby for us. When we went to Mass, we had to fast from midnight the night before, no food, no water, nothing! So after Mass, on my way to school, I always stopped to get something to eat. My friends who didn't go to Mass with me would meet me at Manory's Coffee Shop to get some toast and coffee and maybe some juice before I went to school. Every First Friday we'd meet at Manory's, and every First Friday we'd get our coffee and toast and we'd start smoking, and then we were talking, and then, oh my God, we had missed first period. Well, then we had to wait until second period. And we'd talk some more, and we'd miss—And every month it was the same thing. "Oh my God, it's eleven o'clock. Oh, Father Mulqueen will kill us if we come in now. We'd better not even go in." We missed school every First Friday.

A page from Theresa's high school yearbook, 1953.

In the afternoons, we had to stay off the streets because Father Mulqueen would actually go out looking for truants like us. So every

First Friday afternoon, we went to the deli for bologna, cheese, bread, mustard, and mayonnaise. We'd sneak into the movies and make sandwiches for hours, where Father Mulqueen couldn't find us. When school was out, we came out and joined our school friends at the coffee shop.

I missed a lot of school, not just on First Fridays. I left the house for school every morning, but on the way my friends always seemed to find something else to do. I almost got expelled for missing too many days.

Throughout high school, there was always the influence of the greatest vocation: to become a nun. But honestly, that never even crossed my mind. During our senior year, we had the Vocation Days, and one of the events was to have priests come to talk about how to follow your vocation to be a priest or a nun. We had to sit there and listen to all of that, and the longer I sat there listening, the more nervous I got. "Oh my God," I thought. I suddenly started to feel that God was calling me to become a nun, and I definitely didn't want to do that. During Vocation Day, we were all supposed to see the spiritual director individually. When I went to see him, he asked, "Have you ever thought about being a nun?"

"No," I replied.

"Why not?"

I said, "For one thing, because I like to date, and I smoke, and I love to go out, and I love dancing and partying, and I don't think that goes with being a nun."

He said, "That's true. But, you know, a lot of people have done those things and still go on to be nuns."

I never thought, "Oh, I think I'd like to do that," or, "That sounds nice." It was more like, "Oh my God, I don't want to. Please, don't even let this come back into my mind."

One First Friday morning, we were at Manory's smoking and drinking our coffee like usual when I went to the bathroom. While I was in there washing my hands, a bolt of lightning went through me. Suddenly, I felt this enormous force telling me, "God wants you to be a nun." It sounds absurd, even to me, but it was powerful. I can't explain it. I just knew right then that God was calling me to become a nun. I was shocked, not only because I didn't want to do that, but because I knew that with my conscience, I might actually have to go through with it.

I came out of the restroom and my girlfriends all said, "What's the matter? You look so white. What's wrong?"

I started crying and said, "While I was in there I just got this feeling that God wants me to be a nun."

They said, "Oh my God. Oh, come on."

But then they said, "Well, you do have that kind of holy side to you. Maybe it *was* God? But, no, you're always smoking!"

I felt like all my contradictions were coming out. I didn't want to hear it. I thought, "I'm not going to do this."

I kept trying to dismiss it but I couldn't. I graduated from high school. I was going steady with someone at the time and started working at the college near our home, Rensselaer Polytechnic Institute, as a kind of a clerk/secretary. But the thought that God wanted me to be a nun would not leave me.

Then, one day, I had a flash of insight. I thought of the story in the Bible about Abraham and Isaac, where God told Abraham, "You have to sacrifice your son," and Abraham didn't want to do it. When he finally gave up his son, God stopped him and said, "I was just testing you." So I thought, "That's what it is! He's just testing me to see if I'll do it." I was so relieved.

I went to talk to a priest in the parish. I thought, "If I do the steps, just like Abraham did with Isaac, then God will see that I've tried, and I'll pass his test." That was my only motivation for actually following the steps toward becoming a nun.

The priest had just been ordained, and he was brand new to the parish. This was great for my plan—I figured I would go and talk to him, and when I got the word that I didn't have to go to the convent, it would all go away. I didn't plan on telling anyone I was even thinking of this, and Father Vaughan didn't know my family. It was perfect. I would talk to the priest, but I wouldn't tell him about the test. I just had to follow through the way God wanted me to.

I went to see him, and I said, "I'm thinking of entering the convent."

"Oh, all right. And what order were you thinking about?"

I hadn't thought of any order. We had Sisters of Mercy here and the Sisters of Charity there and I knew that I didn't want to join those orders. I also didn't want him sending me to somebody local because then my secret would be out. So I really had to think fast. "I don't know, maybe a missionary order." I did not have a clue what that meant, I had just heard the words.

"Oh, a missionary," he said. "What about Maryknoll?"

I said, "Oh yeah!" I was like a little actress, and a deceitful one at that. "Yeah, that sounds like the right one." So he gave me some information about Maryknoll. "Why don't you take this home and read it? See what you think about it."

The only thing that I liked about Maryknoll was that its convent was far away from our home. Therefore, I could proceed as if I were interested, ultimately tell them I wasn't going, and my family would be none the wiser. At this point, only my best friends and my boyfriend knew about my "calling."

So I wrote to Maryknoll for an interview. I answered all their questions, and they replied, "We don't think you've given this enough thought, so we're going to reject you coming in."

I was on my way to Lake George when I got this letter. There we go, I thought. Isaac and Abraham. I'd done it!

But there was a bit more to the letter. "However, these are the steps that we think you should be taking." They told me to go to Mass every morning and to join the Legion of Mary, along with a list of other things. I believed that God was telling me that I wasn't off the hook just yet, so I had to follow the steps they set out for me. For an entire year, I did everyhing Maryknoll had asked of me. I set up another interview the following summer.

I went to Maryknoll, still hoping that the nun was going to say, "Obviously, you still haven't given this enough thought."

But she liked everything that I said.

"Okay, you can enter. Would you like to enter in September?"

My stomach sank. Then I thought, "Well, I'll just get it over with," because I knew, I knew that God was not going to make me go in. So I replied, "Oh yes, that would be good, September would be great."

Theresa, 1953.

That night, I was sick to my stomach. I knew God would let me off the hook and that I was close to completing his test, but I was also being pulled further into the convent. I was vomiting all night. I had to come back and tell my parents something that they'd never heard me even talk about. "I'm going into the convent in September." Of course, they accepted this with grace as good Catholics should.

When I saw the list of the items I needed—all these black clothes, black stockings and black shoes and long underwear and horrible stuff and a big black trunk—I was sick to my stomach. I was sick almost every day that summer I was getting ready to enter the convent.

My mother, one of the two times in my life that she ever gave me advice, said, "I don't think you should still be seeing Ed. I don't think it's very fair to him that you're still going out with him all the time."

As it was, I went out with Ed until the night before I left. He was absolutely devastated. He told me he was going to come down and throw rocks at my window in the convent. He was sure that I was going to come out. There was no way that I was going to stay in.

September 2 finally came, and it was time for me to go. I smoked right up to the last minute, all the way down in the car. My parents came with me. Ed wanted to drive me down but my father said, "No, I think that might be pushing it a little bit too much."

Nobody said to me, "You seem unhappy about this." God was asking, so we didn't question it.

So I entered the convent.

CHAPTER 2

Becoming a Maryknoll Sister

When we reached the convent, a bright, cheery young woman in her habit came out and said, "Welcome! We're so glad to have you. I'm Sister Maura Jude, your guardian angel. I'm the person who is going to watch out for you and teach you what to do." She seemed so full of life and joy, and I was relieved to be greeted by such a rich, vibrant nun so unlike the ones I had known at school.

Before she brought me upstairs to the convent dormitory to put on my new clothes, she told my family that they could wait in the chapel, and that we would be back down in a few minutes. I put on those horrible clothes—the black stockings and shoes, the black postulant dress and the little veil. It was strange, but I didn't feel afraid anymore. I didn't feel like I belonged there forever, exactly, but I was no longer sick with nerves. As soon as I put on those black clothes, I remembered how important prayer, and the ritual of prayer, had been for me throughout my life. I was still concerned, but at that moment I felt that I was prepared to stay for a while, even if it was only a few weeks.

Parting with my family was bittersweet. Upon seeing me in my black clothes, they felt enormous Catholic pride that one of their own had been called as God's chosen bride. But at the same time, I was no longer just theirs—we all had the feeling that I somehow no longer belonged to them.

After my family left, I was brought into the chapel to join all the new postulants in prayer. I made a promise to myself and to God that I would never doubt my vocation and that I would really commit to this life, not just for two weeks, but forever. I had only been there for a few minutes, but I had already changed. I felt that I knew that God wanted me to stay in the convent, and I didn't want to doubt him. I would just have to condition myself to this life.

Fifty-two young women entered the convent that day. They were between eighteen and twenty-eight years old, but the majority were nineteen or twenty. All of us were pretty much in the same boat: we were all in a new place, in new clothes, experiencing the same doubts and mixed feelings. It was reassuring. To my surprise, everyone, even the nuns, was normal and vibrant, really fun to be around. There was an air of giddy nervousness in the air as we were led to our dormitories, our "cell blocks." Each individual bed area was called a cell. There were curtains around the beds, similar to what you'd see in a hospital. We each had a single bed, a locker where we kept all of our clothes, and a chair that doubled as a towel rack. The curtains could close around the beds, but we were told that we were not allowed to have the curtains closed at any time, except when we were getting dressed. For the rest of the day, the curtains had to be open. We were supposed to enter into the feeling of community. It felt sort of like entering boarding school.

The next morning, we all went down to unpack our trunks and bring our stuff upstairs. Everything was very scheduled and orderly. The nuns who were training us were very aware of the fact that we were going through a lot of changes, and the training was done with a great deal of sensitivity even though we were immediately told the rules, which were very strict on silence. We were not allowed to talk for much of the day, not even at meals. We would only be allowed to talk during short recreation periods after lunch and dinner. They did let us talk for the first couple of days while we were adjusting. We quickly started orientation classes, which outlined exactly what would be expected of us as postulants. For instance, we were told that we were never to walk around without a veil and our full habit. We even had special night veils that we had to wear when we were getting ready for bed. Although the restrictions were rather severe, the spirit in which things were taught was so human and compassionate that these rules didn't seem so harsh. We all felt fairly normal and joyful in spite of all of the things that were new and strange to us. The rules did make us feel a bit silly from time to time, as if we were children again.

The other postulants were nothing like I had expected. Most of them had dated a lot, had boyfriends, and some had even considered marriage. I'll never forget Dolores Smiskoll. During the first months, we wore postulant veils that allowed the hair around our faces to show. Dolores's hair was so clearly bleached blonde, and who ever heard of a bleached blonde nun? Another had been a model before entering the convent. Some of these girls were really crazy and full of the devil, which was a welcome and refreshing surprise. Many of them were college graduates from fairly sophisticated backgrounds, yet we all seemed to adjust and fit in together very well. For the first month or so, it really wasn't so bad. We had fun, and we were often rather childish and little-girlish.

One example that comes to mind was Saint Theresa's Day. Our superior's name was Sister Miriam Therese, and the superior's feast day was a big occasion to celebrate. We learned a song that we composed ourselves. When I look back at it, the song seems so silly, so juvenile, but that was how we were. The song goes like this:

> On September 2, we came in our finery
> By bus and by train and by special delivery.
> We didn't know a single thing of convent life and such
> Our high heels were changed for some good old ground grippers.
> We fumble with snaps now instead of with zippers,
> Our curly locks pressed under the black veil
> Which calls us postulants.
> (Then the chorus:)
> At Maryknoll, at Maryknoll, we are happy as can be.
> One month old and good as gold
> At least we try to be . . .

Life in the convent was very structured. The day began promptly at five fifteen. After getting ourselves ready and tidying our "cells," we went down for half an hour of meditation and to say our Divine Office, the special prayers we repeated from morning till night. Then we went to Mass and communion, and very often a second Mass before breakfast.

After breakfast, from eight thirty to nine o'clock, we did our charges, which meant that we cleaned and maintained a specific area of the convent that was assigned to us. From nine o'clock to noon, we did whatever our assigned work was for the day—in the beginning, that meant a lot of classes about religious life and how to be a better, holier, more perfect nun. At noon, we went to the dining room, called the refectory, for lunch.

We followed a rule of silence; from five fifteen until after lunch, there were no conversations allowed. After lunch, from twelve thirty to one, we had a recreation period so we could finally talk and go for a walk.

At one o'clock, we went back to classes or work until five, then back to the chapel for more prayers before dinner, which was another silent meal. After dinner, we had one hour of recreation before we returned to the chapel for night prayers. I often stayed later in the chapel and said extra prayers. I was still deeply conflicted about my place in the convent, and I felt I needed all the help I could get. I thought maybe I wasn't really giving myself completely to God and that was why I still had doubts. I strove for more and more perfection, hoping that if I were more generous with God, my conflicts would be resolved. I was always looking for ways to be more devoted, to give more of myself, thinking maybe then I could find some peace and conviction in my vocation.

At nine o'clock, we had what we called "profound silence." There was nothing that was considered important enough to say after nine. We went to bed at nine, lights off at nine thirty. The silence really was profound.

At first, we all had some trouble adjusting to religious life. All of the things that I had never thought twice about before I entered were suddenly different. For example, when we wrote home, all of our letters were censored by the superiors, and we sometimes had to rewrite them if they were deemed unacceptable. One of moments when I realized how different my life was going to be was the first visiting Sunday, when my parents and my former boyfriend came to see me. My girlfriends had told me he was distraught, but it felt different to see it in person. There was a mixture of tension and sadness in breaking away from these things from my old life, things I missed. I remember the first Saturday night, up on the rooftop deck, watching a young couple in a convertible pass by on the country road that went through Westchester. I remember saying to Linda O'Brien, one of the postulants, "Oh my God, it's Saturday night and I don't even have a date."

She looked at me, astounded, and said, "Well, it's not the first Saturday night of *my* life that I haven't had a date. I don't know about you."

It wasn't the first Saturday night of my life either, but I almost always went out on Saturday nights, so there was a pang of sadness when I realized that would no longer be part of my life. I remember feeling the immenseness of this realization, not only of the momentary idea of not being able to go out, but of the thought, "This is the rest of my life." That pang stayed with me the entire time I was at Maryknoll. Even though there were many other wonderful aspects of life in Maryknoll, somehow I was never able to quite get used to the fact that I would never again go out, date, go dancing, or anything else like that.

The first Advent was particularly difficult. It was our first Christmas away from home, and we were unable to write to our families for four weeks. Visitors weren't allowed either. I missed spending Christmas at home terribly. I missed my family, I missed my friends, my social life, the Christmas preparations and everything that went along with that. Christmas preparations in the convent focused on spiritual preparation, which meant spending even more time in prayer and isolation.

Even though it was a very difficult period, I was learning so many new things about myself, about life, and about a host of other topics that I had never studied before. I also made very close friends with some of the other girls, and I really enjoyed their company. They were entertaining, witty, and wonderful. Little by little, we were broken into what religious life was all about. I was becoming acclimated. I began to feel the richness of life at Maryknoll, and I felt a real strength coming into me. It was overwhelming to be around so many people who were so incredibly committed to their aspirations, and I was inspired and enriched by my own feelings of idealism. Even though I entered the convent out of a sense of fear, I had always had an idealistic strain and a strong desire to do and be good. Maryknoll nourished a lot of that, and it also gave me insight into the greater purpose of being a human being. I learned that life should be about discovering the world around me and struggling to make that world a better place. I developed an inner richness, an inner spirituality. For the whole twelve years that I stayed in Maryknoll, this richness was the most integral part of my experience. I was incredibly happy on many levels. But there was always an ache of wanting to go out and have a social life, to go on dates and, eventually, get marrried and have a large family. I never lost my desire for all of that. Yet, simultaneously, I loved Maryknoll and everything I was learning about people, life, and the world. I was constantly trying to achieve some semblance of balance between these two opposing desires, but I never really could, not fully.

For the first nine months in Maryknoll, we were called postulants. We hadn't yet taken any vows. It was mostly a learning period. It was around this time that many people left because they were too homesick or because they just couldn't stand it any longer.

After that, we spent one year as novices in a place called Lady

Crest in Topsfield, Massachusetts. Lady Crest was much stricter. We couldn't see our families for a whole year, and most of that time was spent praying, working, and "silencing." It was more intense, and we were much more isolated.

I went up into the hills of Topsfield aware of the two levels that I was living on. One level was God's will, which I was trying to do, and which I had to remind myself was what I wanted. The other level was me, my personal desires and fears. I felt that my goal was to increasingly merge the "me" level into the "God" level so that they would be one, and I would no longer have to be stuck between the two parts of myself. Any time a superior asked me if I was struggling, if I missed my life outside, I had to convince myself to dismiss these ideas and say, "No, really, this is what God wants for me, and this is what I truly want." I was afraid that if I were honest about it, I would be betraying God. But I felt that I was always struggling within myself. Perhaps if I had been truthful, I would have gotten the help that I needed. Most of the nuns that I lived with had no idea I was feeling this way. In general, I was very outgoing and happy, and it seemed that I had adjusted to religious life so well that many years later, when I did leave, people were astounded. I was becoming the perfect nun. The more I struggled against myself, the more perfect I tried to become to counteract it.

During the year at Topsfield, the superior was watching all the novices very closely. Often, people were asked to leave if the superior didn't feel that they were right for Maryknoll. I was always hoping that I would be told to leave, but at the same time, I was doing everything perfectly, because I couldn't intentionally offend God.

When the canonical year ended, I returned to the motherhouse as a senior novice, ready to welcome new postulants into the convent. We were now the guardian angels tasked with showing new girls how to adjust to religious life and become good nuns.

Throughout our second year as novices, we were building toward taking our first vows. In our religious life classes, we learned about the different types of vows: the vow of poverty, the vow of chastity, and the vow of obedience. The vow of poverty, of course, meant that, although our basic needs were well taken care of, we would relinquish all possessions; nothing belonged to us individually, but instead belonged to the community. We were not allowed to accept any gifts; if our parents brought gifts for Christmas or birthdays, we had to give them to the superior. If we felt we had a right or a need to keep a certain gift, such as a pen, we had to write a note asking for permission. The superior would then talk with us and determine whether we really needed it. The vow of poverty, in part, was to relieve us of all material goods and the responsibility toward them so that we could focus our time and attention on spiritual matters. When we felt that our clothing was ready to be disposed of, we had to put it in the superior's basket with a note requesting new clothes. The superior made the final decisions about these things, and if she felt that you could still get some use out of them, she returned them and told you to wear them for a while longer.

The vow of chastity implied not only the absence of sexual relationships or intimacy, but total devotion of yourself to God—you were marrying yourself to him. From that oneness with him, you had to extend yourself, your energy, your love, your concern, and your affection to all of his creation, so that instead of caring about your husband or children as others would, you had to put all of that energy into the world and care for everyone equally. This included the idea of not having particular friendships. We were supposed to have a positive attitude about celibacy, to celebrate it instead of dwelling on what we were giving up.

The vow of obedience meant total submission to the orders of the superior. If you felt you might be a better doctor than a teacher, or that you would be better prepared to serve in China than in South America because of certain gifts that you thought you had, then you could bring it up, but you were never to expect that the superior would heed your request. Very often, the superior would decide just the opposite of what you felt you needed. This has greatly changed in Maryknoll from what I understand, but at the time we were told what to do and to accept that God's will came through the voice of the superior. Part of this obedience meant that, even if the superior made a mistake, you were not making a mistake by carrying out what the superior told you to do.

June 24, the day when we took our vows, was coming near. This was to be the most serious commitment yet, and I was struggling with the decision. With these vows, I would be committing myself for one full year, and the formula would be similar to the final vows we were expected to eventually take. It wasn't as though I was constantly overwhelmed, but there were periods when it became unbelievably difficult, especially when I thought about making another, more formal commitment to God. When we took our first vows, I was to say: "I, Sister Maura Killene (my religious name), do hereby vow poverty, chastity, and obedience to God, to the Blessed Virgin Mary, to our Holy Father St. Dominic, and to all the saints." Each year until we took our final vows, we took a different vow. I was torn to pieces each time I spoke my vows, wondering how I could possibly say these words when I was still so torn about meaning them.

I went through the ceremony of first vows and cried all night, wondering whether I would ever convince myself that this was what I wanted to do, promising myself always that I would try even harder to dismiss all of my doubts and live better. I was working harder and harder to become the perfect nun. Some of my best friends from the postulant days were saying, "God, what's happening? You're getting so serious at times, looking so holy." But we were not supposed to discuss our doubts with one another, so I shared very little with my friends. In some ways, I felt like I was laughing on the outside and crying on the inside. Then again, I was also really enjoying what I was learning and doing at Maryknoll, and it wasn't as though I was in a state of constant suffering and confusion.

After I took my temporary vows, I went to the superior, Sister Loretta, and said, "I think I made a mistake."

"What do you mean?" she asked.

"I don't think I want to be here. I think I made a mistake."

"Well, what do you think is causing this? You've been here this long, and you're doing so well."

I said, "I don't think I—I just don't think I have wanted to be a nun. I think I thought I had to or something."

She said, "Oh, Sister Maura Killene, you have been such a good nun. This is the devil, you know. These are the temptations that the devil does. Now that you're closer to where you're really going, the devil's going to tempt you all the more."

I started telling the priest in confession the same thing, and I said, "I really often want to just go—I want to get married, I want to have children."

He said, "Those are just temptations. It's very normal. The more you're tempted, the closer you are to God. It means that God has an even more special place for you. He tempts those he loves most." I don't know if I totally bought that. I don't think I did, but I did believe that I was meant to stay there. The temptations just went with the territory. So I stayed.

In 1958, when it came time for my final vows, I dreaded it. Our parents and families came, and there were five hundred people in the chapel. We all went—the thirty-five of us left out of the fifty-two who started—and lined up at the altar. The priest placed a missionary cross around each of our necks and we received our wedding rings to God. When he came to me, he said, "Okay, repeat after me. I, Sister Maura Killene, do hereby vow poverty, chastity, and obedience to God, to the Blessed Virgin Mary, to St. Dominic, for the rest of my life."

The minute I said, "I, Sister Maura Killene," I broke down, sobbing up there at the altar in front of all five hundred people. I could not say the words.

Finally, the priest said, "Are you all right, Sister?" I couldn't respond, so eventually, he said, "Well, okay, I'll say the words and you can just nod your head if it's okay." So he said, "I, Sister Maura Killene . . . Okay?" I kept crying as I nodded my head.

I thought, "Well, certainly it's out that I'm a little bit disturbed about this." When I left the altar, everyone was joyous, hugging each other. It was like a wedding day for many people. I was absolutely devastated.

That's not what other people saw. One of the superiors, who also taught me in psychology class, came up and said, "Oh, Sister Maura Killene, that was so moving. You know, if that had been anybody else but you, I would have thought that there were last-minute doubts, but knowing you and how dedicated you are, I knew that you were just filled with so much emotion on this wonderful day."

Theresa (second from left, front) with her fellow Sisters, late 1950s.

After my profession of vows, I became a professed sister. My first assignment was to be the secretary to the mother general. I had not been terribly academically inclined in high school, but as secretary to the mother general, I excelled. I discovered that I was not stupid by any means, and so long as I had the information I needed to complete a project, I was at least as competent as other people. I worked in the mother general's office for two years.

As professed sisters, we were eligible for assignment to any country in the world. A number of sisters with whom I had entered, particularly those who had been prepared academically before they came in, were sent right out to the missions. For instance, Sister Dolores, my bleached blonde friend, was a nurse, so she went right off to Korea. It was a difficult to watch my friends go knowing I would likely never see them again. Once we were assigned to a specific country, we were expected to stay there for ten years, so the chances of running into these girls again was slim. That summer was an emotional time. In addition to saying goodbye to the people we had grown to know and love, it was also tough to be among the nuns who weren't yet assigned to a mission. Personally, I wasn't dying to go because I was a bit of a coward, unsure if I could handle all the rigors of that life, but there were many nuns who were terribly disappointed every year when the assignments came out and they had not been chosen.

Those of us who remained at the motherhouse learned about the missions and what other nuns and priests were doing in Libya, Peru, Japan, and the rest of the world at dinner readings of diary entries that nuns had sent back to the motherhouse. I was terrified. Nuns wrote about getting ready for bed and seeing a snake curled around the bedpost. In the jungles of Bolivia, a nun said she opened up a drawer and out jumped a tarantula. I was the world's biggest coward, and I was positive that I would be sent somewhere besieged by snakes and spiders and all these other terrible animals. Every night when I went to my clean lily-white bed, I always prayed that I would have the courage to endure my assignment, wherever it may be.

At the same time, the diaries were very inspiring, and many of the nuns who had written them were already on their way back. When they returned to the motherhouse, they told us all about their experiences, and we all noticed how vibrant and joyful the missionaries were when they returned. Stuck in the motherhouse, our worldview became narrower, but the missionaries were out in other countries dealing with village life. Their focus had changed and their perspective had expanded so much. The missionary diaries were meant to help us broaden our worldview and maintain focus on the outside world.

In May of 1960, I was assigned to go to Maryknoll's Mary Rogers College located on the grounds of the motherhouse. Since I had frolicked away my high school years and never gone to college, I was thrilled with the idea and entered with a lot of enthusiasm. My assignment was to prepare to be a teacher, so I majored in education with a minor in philosophy. I was really pleased to find out that I could be a very good student, as it again confirmed for me that I wasn't totally stupid. I enjoyed college a lot. I was loosening up a little bit because I no longer felt that I had to prove something to myself by trying to be the perfect nun. College was a fruitful, positive time for me.

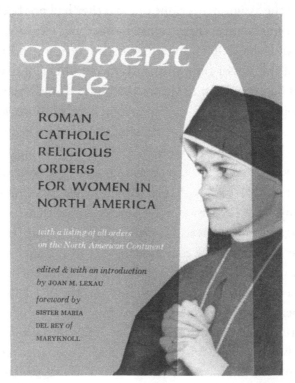

Theresa on the cover of *Convent Life*, 1964.

Senior year was a rough time for all practice teachers. We had to leave the motherhouse in the morning and go into New York City, where we had to take shuttles, buses, and trains to arrive at our destinations. Nuns from other orders sat and evaluated us throughout the day, which was intimidating and difficult. I enjoyed learning how to teach and to stand in front of a classroom. It actually felt good. I was able to impart information and do it in a systematic way, developing relationships on that level. In addition, I was one of the seniors who was asked to go out and teach religion in a nearby public school. The four of us who were chosen were supposed to teach with some of the seminarians. As it turned out, the seminarians were about the same age as we were. We traveled in the same car together, shared many of the same values, and we were all between twenty-three and twenty-five years old. Of course, we were naturally attracted to one another. I was astounded at how free my friend Sister Regina David was. We would get in the car and if she had to sit in someone's lap, she would. I was always more aloof, worried that my ulterior motives would show if I let my guard down.

Assignments came later that spring. Mother General came into the refectory one day, as she did every year on an unknown day, and said, "I have the assignments today." We all sat, listening eagerly as she began reading off the countries. "The following sisters will go to Africa." All of the sisters were jubilant, yelling and crying with joy. Most of the sisters really wanted to go to foreign missions and were happy unless they had wanted to go to a different country. Mother General finally announced my assignment: I, Sister Maura Killene, would be going to Chile. I was happy to go, because I knew I needed to break away from the motherhouse, to experience a drastic change. Maybe this would help me. I was still afraid that I would have to live in a hut somewhere full of snakes and spiders, without running water or anything. Having heard of the rugged life that many of the other missionaries endured, I expected the worst. I immediately started preparing myself to be a good missionary, telling myself that I would get used to it after a while.

On Sunday, we had a big ceremony for the departing nuns out in the grotto at Maryknoll. We had Japanese gardeners who tended to everything, and the grotto was an artistic masterpiece. The priests announced where each of us was going and hung our mission crucifixes around our necks. My entire family came out to see me, and it was all very exciting.

Theresa in habit at home with her parents, 1964.

I went back to my hometown for a week before I left for Chile. I stayed with the nuns in our town at a nearby convent since we weren't allowed to sleep in our own homes with our families, but I was able to visit my family during the day. I showed them some films about South America and tried to tell them what I would be doing. I also had to recruit sponsors to send me money every month for the mission. It was all very exhilarating, but as the time approached to say goodbye, I felt as if it was the first time in my life that I truly understood what people meant when they said that this was the time when you pull up your roots. I felt as if every bone, every muscle, and every sinew in my body was being uprooted. It felt as if someone had taken out everything that was inside of me. But I knew that if I was going to this new country—this new life—that I had to get rid of everything I felt. It was a very strange feeling. I felt sad and sick at heart, but at the same time, I felt a great deal of exhilaration.

Invitation to the sixtieth mission departure, 1964.

CHAPTER 3

A Maryknoller in Chile
and My Decision to Leave

The day finally came when the four of us assigned to Chile em-
barked on a freighter, the *Copiapó*. We were on the boat for twenty-
one days, stopping at different cities along the way. It was the first
time I had gotten to leave the motherhouse and intermingle with
the laity. There was a young man on the boat who, of course, distracted me, but there were just so many people and things to be
distracted by. I really enjoyed being around people other than nuns,
even if I did get seasick.

On the ship to Chile, 1964.

The regional superior of Chile was there with another nun to greet us as we got off the ship and went through customs. After customs, we went off with the nuns, immediately entering an exclusively Spanish-speaking environment. I had been with Spanish-speaking people for the entire twenty-one-day voyage, but somehow getting off the boat made everything seem new and different.

I had really tried to mentally prepare myself for the rigors I imagined this kind of life entailed—the poverty, the hardship. Much to my amazement, on our way out there, we stopped in a gorgeous, elegant restaurant which wasn't quite like the image of mission life we had in our minds.

Theresa and children in Pucón, Chile, 1964.

From there we drove to Buceta, a place in Santiago, Chile. I was expecting to see a very rustic convent, or perhaps a hut like I had seen in the pictures of places that some of our other missionaries worked. Although the convent was not terribly homey or attractive, it was certainly far from being a hut. When we got there, we met a number of sisters, perhaps fifteen, who were living in Santiago. They all came over to have dinner with us and we had a wonderful time talking with them all.

We stayed at the convent for a week or two to visit the school and neighborhood and see what the nuns were doing. Everything was so new and exciting. We got to stay to see the inauguration of Eduardoo Frei as president of Chile before moving on toward our final destination.

Theresa on a boat during her *Gran Misión,* 1964.

After that, we started on the road down through Chile, past the other missions, toward Pucón, which was five hundred miles south of Santiago. On our way down, we stopped at a few of the convents and missions in the country. As we arrived at each new convent, the sisters would prepare a special dinner to welcome us to Chile. I enjoyed seeing their different activities being carried out, watching the different types of work that they did, and visiting all the people in the villages.

Those of us who came to Chile at that time were referred to as the "new breed" because we had been prepared to enter the mission with a different attitude than the nuns that came before us. At the time, Pope John XXIII had just "opened all the windows of the churches," as everyone was saying, and started breathing new life and vitality into the church. There was a new belief that we should be going out and meeting with the people directly instead of staying in our convents. We had always been taught that we had to "be in the world, not of it," but Pope John was indicating the opposite, that it wasn't right to stay stuck in our ivory towers and our fifteenth-century clothing. As the theologians began carrying out everything Pope John was saying, we began to feel a very wonderful and vibrant spirit enter the church that affected religious life very deeply. The older nuns used to joke that they were afraid of us and the ideas we would bring. It was a joyful time for us.

I had been assigned to go far out in the country to Galvarino, and then even further into the mountains for a two-week *Gran Misión*. I had never ridden a horse before, and I was very nearly thrown off! We worked with the indigenous people and a group of rich girls from the affluent schools nearby. We hoped that by bringing them out into the mountains, we could educate them on the needs of their own people. In addition, the two groups shared their religious education. I had only been in the country for about six weeks, but I was already being introduced to experiences that were generally reserved for sisters who had been in the country much longer. This was supposed to be a privilege, but I had very mixed feelings about going to the mountains, where I had heard there was absolutely no plumbing and animals wandering all over the place. I went to Galvarino with a great deal of trepidation, always anticipating things to be much worse than they ultimately turned out to be.

For the first couple of days, a cart pulled by two *buey*, or oxen, carried us through the mountains. They took us up extremely narrow roads where we could look over the precipice and down the side of the mountain. The *campesino*, or farmer, hitting the *bueys* with a little stick was the only thing keeping us from falling right off. It was terrifying, yet within three days I felt acclimated—I was actually enjoying my experience immensely.

In some ways, living in the mountains was basically what I'd expected. The building that we lived in was completely open, like a big hall, and we slept on flour bags filled with straw. Chicken and sheep were always running around the farm, which was right outside, making noise all night. We had no running water, no bathrooms, no sinks—nothing. When we had to go to the bathroom, we went outside in the bushes. In the morning, we were led to a hollowed-out tree trunk filled with water from the mountains with a dirty rag hanging on the side, and this was supposed to be our sink. To my amazement, I loved seeing how the people adapted to it.

Every afternoon, we spent three or four hours walking through the mountains, through the hills, and visiting little cardboard huts, telling the *campesinos* when to come down to the schoolhouse. The next morning, we would hold classes at nine o'clock in the center house.

I believe this was was probably the most transformative experience of my life. Much of what I care about today has its roots in those two weeks in Chile, when we went up the hills to arrive at people's homes where they had nothing—absolutely nothing—yet they always found a way to go out and find a peach in a tree or eggs laid by their hens to give to us. Sometimes they gave us some *mate*, an herb drink that always scalded my mouth and stomach to pieces. We always accepted these gestures of hospitality no matter what they offered. They used tree trunks as tables, and they would spread clean flour sacks on top of them when serving guests. It seemed so elegant under the circumstances. They were so wonderful to us.

We saw their poverty and sickness and the way the *patróns*, their bosses, treated them. Some of them were afraid to come down to the mission because their bosses wouldn't allow them the day off.

Mothers of four or five little children were forced to leave them alone in those little shacks all day while they went to work in the fields with their husbands, fearing that the *patrón* would fire them if they didn't. Seeing all of this greatly impacted me. I didn't know it yet, but I had been thrown right into what would later become one of the most important causes in my life.

In spite of all the hardships, I was so touched by all my new experiences that I soon forgot the physical difficulties that initially terrified me.

Even though I had studied two years of Spanish in college and was fairly good at it, I was far from fluent enough to survive in Chile, so they sent me to the language school in Pucón. I was there with Sister Rose Carol, who was later killed in El Salvador. The superior wanted to experiment with a new way of teaching Spanish: we would be completely isolated for six months to a year, only listening to language tapes and reading Spanish books until we mastered the language. This was possibly the most miserable way in the world to learn a new language. Pucón was a little town, perhaps six blocks by six blocks, where nothing exciting ever happened. During the summer it was a vacation resort, but during the winter it was almost totally abandoned. With the exception of our housekeeper, our gardener, and one elderly lady who lived there and came in to talk to us each day for an hour or two, we were on our own, focusing on learning Spanish. It wasn't fun, but we did improve greatly.

In Pucón, it rained horrendously for nine months, so for most of the year, we couldn't go out. It was so cold that our bathroom served as a makeshift refrigerator. We did our best to acclimate to the freezing cold, but neither of us ever really got used to the lack of central heating and the bad electricity.

Sister Rose Carol and I kept each other sane. She was one of those wonderfully creative and poetic people, and we devoured every magazine we could get our hands on, Spanish or English, it didn't matter. When we felt ourselves going totally crazy, we would take a tape recorder and tape ourselves performing little plays and acts. I used to pretend I was Mother Superior. In a lot of ways, Pucón was horrible, but Sister Rose Carol and I had such a hilarious time trying to remain sane when we felt like we were going crazy. It was like Sartre's *No Exit*.

After our time in Pucón, I was assigned to Talcahuano, Chile, to work at a high school in the region. I was surprised because brand new language students were usually placed in grade schools or parishes, not high schools, until they had a better grasp of the language. High school students are much more aware of any mistakes their new teacher may be making, and they tend to be a bit more critical. The general consensus seemed to be that I had achieved a pretty good fluency rate and was ready to take on the high school job.

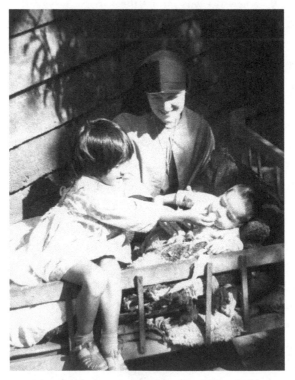

Theresa playing with children in Chile, 1964.

The convent in Talcahuano was very beautiful, perhaps the nicest in all of Chile. The priests lived a block away from us in the rectory. In addition to a high school, there was a grade school, a sewing school, a vocational school, and a commercial school. Maryknoll ran the entire compound. Factories surrounded us, so we were exposed to a cross section of the entire community. Within the parish, there were the owners and administrators of the factories, as well as laborers down to the lowest rung. There were pockets of wealth and pockets of poverty all mixed in together.

For my first assignment, I had a class of students from seventh-graders to high school seniors. I taught religion and English on all levels, and on occasion, I also taught typing, counseling, and something that was called "religious formation." I really loved what I was doing, even though I was a new teacher and the whole concept of the lesson plan was still unfamiliar to me. It was difficult at first, but I was sure I could do it, and that encouraged me. I was also inspired by the new spirit of the church, thanks to Pope John XXIII, which encouraged us to get out and get involved with the people. Outside of my classes, I spent a lot of time with the people of the parish. I was overwhelmed by the poverty and misery I saw in so many places, and by the wealth disparity within the community. One day I'd be at one end of the parish in someone's gorgeous, luxurious home, and the next day I'd be at the other end of the parish where the people didn't have central heating, medical care, or even beds. It really was a lot to take in.

As I mentioned, at the time I was in Talcahuano, Chile, Pope John XXIII had been appealing for new changes within the church to enable us to become more alive and aware, but he had also inaugurated a new approach to the way priests and nuns would work together. Despite often working in the same parishes, there had always been a great deal of separation between priests and nuns. The priests acted as directors while we worked under them in whatever capacity the parish required.

By 1965, many of these things were changing. There was a new emphasis on working together with the priests, and even interacting socially with them. The regional superior, who was in charge of all the sisters in Chile, suggested that we invite them over for dinner on special occasions. Sister Vincent DePaul, the local superior at the time, was very uncomfortable with this. She was a wonderful woman in many ways, but this much change terrified her. In retrospect, I admire her ability to open up and allow the changes to take place in spite of her fears.

Theresa with children on her *Gran Misión*, 1967.

That said, Sister Vincent DePaul did struggle to adjust, and she had a particularly hard time opening up to Father Braun. He could be abrasive, but he was so bright and energetic, so full of ideas. I found him inspiring. He had a particular talent for organizing youth groups. The best example of this was when Father Braun managed to get all of us nuns into a movie theater with local college and high school students, and then into a discussion group—for a movie we weren't even allowed to see! Up until then, movies had been screened in the convent, and we could only watch very mild movies like *The Sound of Music*. We were not allowed to go to a theater with other people. This was just beginning to change while we were down there. Our regional superior was very liberal, and our local superior was trying her best to adapt to the changes, but, as I mentioned, she was having a hard time with it. When Sister Vincent DePaul was away for the week, Father Braun called us up at the convent and said that *Zorba the Greek* was playing in the theater, and invited us to see it with him and our youth groups from high school and college. Afterward, he said we would have a *cine foro*, which is something like a discussion group.

It was incredible. We were still in our long habits—veils and all—and stood out everywhere we went, especially in a movie theater with a priest. I was astounded that he suggested we come along with him, especially with the students. There were some fairly racy scenes in *Zorba the Greek*, and the students were embarrassed sitting with us, which embarrassed us as well. After the film, we all went back to the parish hall and held a discussion with the students. Father Braun thought *Zorba* was marvelous. I don't remember too many details about the movie, but I remember that I was still prudish enough to feel that there was a bit too much sex. Because there was a scene with a prostitute, I didn't think that Zorba should be looked upon as the Great, the Marvelous, the Wonderful, or whatever. Father Braun, on the other hand, was practically painting him as Zorba the Saint, saying that he represented the complete person. I disagreed, but the discussion continued.

When Sister Vincent DePaul came back, she overheard us discussing *Zorba*. She was horrified and angry with us. She couldn't believe that we would see this type of movie at all, let alone with the "children" from the parish! Not to mention that we saw it with Father Braun, whom she could not tolerate. Sister Helen Frederick, who had known Sister Vincent DePaul for many years and was a close friend of hers, got a kick out of seeing her in such hysterics. "Oh, Sister, don't be such a prude. You should have gone to the movie yourself," she teased. To us, she said, "Remember that scene where they were all running down to the beach with no clothes on?" Sister Vincent DePaul was getting even more anxious and flustered. "You mean you saw scenes like this with the students?" Sister Helen Frederick thougt this was hysterical and continued egging Sister Vincent DePaul on. After that, whenever we wanted to get a jolt out of Sister Vincent DePaul, we brought up *Zorba the Greek*. Months afterward, we still got a kick out of it.

Around the same time, Maryknoll began experimenting with new styles of habits, and word came from the motherhouse that any of the sisters who felt ready to change their habits should consult with their local superiors. There were three or four of us who were raring to "modify our habits," as it was called. We went to the parish seamstresses, who designed our new uniform: a very businesslike gray suit, sandal shoes, and a little veil. We were so excited to get out of the old garb and look more normal. It was exhilarating.

I loved Latin America. I admired the whole attitude about life, the importance placed on taking time to connect with one another. When we entered a room saying, "Good morning, how are you?" and went straight to work, like we did in the States, they would stop us and say, "Wait a minute. Do you care how I'm doing or not? You ask, but are you going to wait and listen?" It was amazing how much they taught us.

Another thing I appreciated was the difference between Latin men and American men. Even in my full habit, when talking to a Latin man, it always felt like he was looking at me as a woman, not just as a nun, maybe thinking, "Hey, you aren't too bad looking." In a way, it felt good to have my femininity acknowledged like that.

It was becoming easier and more acceptable for laypeople to ask more personal questions about our lives in the church. I had a wonderful friend, Ricardo Lama, who I worked with a lot. Although he was handsome, there was no attraction bringing us together, just a strong friendship. I think Ricardo always sensed what I was going through, too. By then, Sister Vincent DePaul had left and I had become principal of the school. Sister Marcella Marie was my new superior. One morning Ricardo, Sister Marcella Marie, and I were having coffee when somehow the discussion came around to our vows. Ricardo came out and asked us, "Isn't it difficult to make a vow of chastity?" A year before, no one would have dared to ask that question. Flustered, Sister Marcella Marie said, "Oh no, of course it isn't difficult at all. Once you've made your vow, that's it. It's all over with."

I was amazed by the quickness of her answer. On the way home, I asked Sister Marcella Marie about her reply. "Did you respond to him like that because you didn't think he had a right to ask you a personal question? I'm curious, why were you so quick and firm in your response?"

She said, "No . . . well, both. First, I don't think it is his business, and second, I was telling the truth. I've never had any problems with chastity. I have never wanted to be married. I love this life and there is absolutely no other life that I have aspired to."

I was astounded. I had been in the convent for ten or eleven years and this was the first time I ever heard anyone say that they didn't have any difficulties with the vow of chastity. I figured that everyone just dealt with their urges by repressing them. I told her I couldn't believe it. It was the first time that I ever opened up to her.

When I told her all the problems I was having with chastity, she said, "You know, I sort of sensed that."

Whenever Sister Marcella Marie and I went into town, she would kid me about what I had revealed in that conversation. Perhaps she sensed that I related to men on a different level than she did, and perhaps I was being too friendly with them. Still, she maintained her wonderful sense of humor about it. "Come on now, keep those eyes where they're supposed to be," she'd laugh. Once, she added thoughtfully, "I think it is pretty strong with you. I don't know how deep it is, or what you're struggling with. Since the day I took my vows, I have never had to struggle with chastity."

As I said, everything was changing for us. Shortly thereafter, we started having what we called "common meditation," where we'd sit around and choose a passage from the gospel and discuss how it applied to our rules. In one of these discussions, the topic of chastity came up. Sister Ann Virginia, who I greatly admired—she must have been forty-five or fifty at the time—concurred with Sister Marcella Marie that she had never wanted to get married, and furthermore, never had any trouble with the rule of chastity. She loved her work and was very involved with the parish. She didn't feel that she was missing out on anything; she was completely fulfilled. I began to realize little by little that not many of the other nuns had any difficulty either.

I started discussing chastity with Sister Ann Virginia. She told me, "You are one of my favorite nuns. I think you have so much potential. You've got so much more energy than most of the other nuns who have ever come to the house. You have so much drive, but I know you're really struggling. I can see it." I thought I was feeling better than ever, and yet my problem was clearly still there, visible to those around me. Then she said, "You know, I don't want to overly influence any of your decisions about the future, but you should know, God doesn't ask the impossible of us."

Sister Ann Virginia was the most helpful person for me at that time, and she ultimately helped me realize I needed to leave Maryknoll. She spoke with me a number of times afterward, always telling me how much I meant to her, and that I was an ideal Maryknoll sister. She advised me to go see a spiritual director, recommending Father Maloney, a psychologist and Maryknoll priest who had recently joined our parish. She also invited me to continue talking with her.

By this time, I was the principal of Corpus Christi and was still teaching and running youth groups. It was absolutely one of the most energetic periods of my life. I couldn't seem to do enough, and

I loved every moment of it. Almost everything I did was my choice, except for becoming the principal, a position to which I had been appointed. This was the peak of my life at that point. I was trying harder than ever to overcome my difficulties because I enjoyed the work aspects of life so much and didn't want to give up anything.

At Christmas 1965, the mother general visited the missions. She was concerned because a nun had left her mission in Guatemala and had married a Maryknoll priest. It was a great shock for Maryknoll. No one could believe it, because as far as we knew, nothing like this had ever happened during the entire history of the church. To make sure that it didn't happen again, the mother general and father general began visiting our missions. I had worked in her office as her secretary, so the mother general knew me personally. While she was there, she told me how proud she was of me.

"You are doing such a fantastic job," she said. "You've been elected to be the chapter delegate from Chile even though you've only been in the country for a year and a half. All the other sisters have so much respect for you."

This was a joyful period for us. We were busy preparing for Christmas Mass, when we would all join the priests for a celebration. When they came over on Christmas Eve, one of the priests played the guitar, and we sang Christmas songs and had an all-around merry time.

Before Mass, I went up to my cell. In the mission convents, each nun had her own private room, but they were still called "cells." We had our own bed, a beautiful large desk, bookshelves, and our own little sink. It was very luxurious and far more private than the motherhouse had been. I was exhilarated by everything that was going on. I was learning new skills and discovering skills I didn't even know I had. But when I went into my cell that night and closed the door, I suddenly burst into tears. I didn't know where this was coming from. I had been feeling so wonderful just a moment before, and all of a sudden an immense feeling of loneliness seemed to rise up from the pit of my stomach. It was the most unusual experience that I think I ever had. Externally, everything about me seemed so vibrant, but this feeling was like an empty, empty hole, and I couldn't seem to get a hold of it. I couldn't understand why this was happening to me now, when I was becoming so alive, so aware, and so happy. And after I thought I finally had things under control.

Later at Midnight Mass, everything was so cheerful. All the parishioners were saying "Merry Christmas" to one another and everyone was flocking over to us because the mother general was there. It was so wonderful, but I couldn't get rid of my loneliness. When we went into the church and sat down together—the nuns usually sat in the front of the chapel—and Mass began, I felt everything just surging up inside of me. Finally, I had to go sit by myself because I could no longer restrain the tears. I didn't want anyone to see the tears rolling down my face, so I walked by myself to the convent and went up to my cell where I just cried and cried.

I was still crying when I heard all the nuns coming back from Midnight Mass. It was our custom after Mass to have a candlelight procession in the convent and then to have hot chocolate and donuts. Sister Patricia Mary came up to my cell to see if I was all right.

Sister Patricia Mary and I were very close friends, and we were both struggling with our vocations. That night we talked for a long while about everything going on inside us.

This was definitely the beginning of the end, though I prefer to think of it as the beginning of the beginning. I was approaching my life with new intensity and purpose, but the anguish and loneliness would not leave me.

On Sister Ann Virginia's recommendation, I began seeing a psychiatrist, but at this point, I was grasping for anything. In weekly sessions, I told him about my problems with temptations against my vocation. He was a very good listener, and it helped to finally talk about what I had been feeling, but I desperately needed somebody's input. Sister Ann Virginia's counsel was more like what I needed at that time, but I kept going to the psychiatrist for professional help and for his prodigious listening skills.

I had been elected chapter delegate for the region, which meant I was to be one of the two sisters from Chile who would visit the motherhouse every four years to meet with chapter delegates from other countries to discuss issues and ideas raised by other missionary nuns. It was considered a very big honor. Part of my job was to travel from Talcahuano to the center house in Santiago. I had to leave at midnight to arrive at six in the morning, switching buses three times along the way, which always made me sick to my stomach and desperately nauseous.

In Santiago, we discussed community problems and the direction Maryknoll was heading. It seemed increasingly incongruous to me that I was the person elected to discuss Maryknoll's new path, while I was becoming acutely aware that I had to leave.

Whenever I visited the center house in Santiago, where Regional Superior Sister Stephanie Marie lived, I would call upon my good friend Sister Margaret Frances who was secretary of the chapter meetings. Like me, she would later leave Maryknoll. Today, she is married and has two children, and we're still close friends. At the time, however, she was having the same struggle I was, so we used to meet to discuss our anxieties.

Because I was under considerable stress, I began smoking again. My friends Sonia, Rosa, and Estrella came to the convent, and we met in the guest room where we locked all the doors and opened the windows so I could smoke like crazy.

Sister Margaret Frances had also started smoking. Whenever we met, it was apparent that both of us were starting to crack up. Every night I would alternate between blistering hot flashes and freezing in my perspiration. It was as though I were going through menopause. My anxiety was finally exhibiting itself through physical symptoms. I also had a terrible case of anemia at the time because we didn't have any blood donation programs in Chile. Any time someone in the parish needed blood transfusions, they went to the parishioners with the same blood type. It seemed as though I was always running down to give blood. My anemia became so severe that I had to go to the doctor several times and take iron pills, which turned out to be a blessing in disguise because it forced me to go to a doctor who started giving me other medicine. I blinded myself to the real meaning behind that. I had never really taken pills, so when the doctor prescribed medicine, I was somehow under the impression it was meant to treat anemia. I didn't know that they were tranquilizers.

At chapter meetings, Sister Margaret Frances and I would go to the bathroom during lunch hour, get out our cigarettes and smoke up a storm even though the smell of smoke clung to the walls. Somehow, the worse things became, the funnier they seemed, at least to us. Sister Margaret Frances was so sick and nervous that she developed ulcers, so she was constantly belching. We sat in the bathroom laughing our heads off, puffing away like two fanatics. While she belched, I pulled out another cigarette, and another after that. We just couldn't believe that we were going crazy. Back in the meetings, everyone held me in high esteem as though I were "Miss Maryknoll Sister," the perfect nun, deciding new directions for Maryknoll.

At the same time, there were more and more changes happening in our order, and more rules were being lifted. We were finally allowed to listen to regular music. Sister Margaret Frances and two other nuns had a record by the Sandpipers, and one of the songs on the album was "Guantanamera." After chapter meetings, they put on their record and danced around the living room. We had never been able to do this before. I loved "Guantanamera" so much. It was just so beautiful. It was about revolution, but I wasn't a politicized person yet, so the song didn't really have any political connotations for me. Instead, I admired the message of taking responsibility for one's actions in life. On top of that, I had read *Siddartha* and was greatly influenced by the book's call to take charge of my life and decisions. Whenever I read *Siddartha* or listened to "Guantanamera," something would come over me and I would think, *"I've got to make* the change! *I've* got to do it! *I've* got to risk it!" I felt joyful and determined and began to feel some strength come back.

I was visiting the doctor periodically for my anemia. The doctor examined me and my blood samples and said, "You know, you're fine now. The anemia is completely under control and you're back to normal. But there's clearly still something seriously wrong, and I think you better try to deal with it." I was so rigid about my rules and my commitment to God and to the order that I didn't think it was appropriate for me to discuss my problems with the doctor. But he continued, "Sister, you know you're in perfectly good shape physically. But you have to make some kind of a decision soon or you're not going to be in good mental shape."

"What do you mean?" I asked him defensively.

"Every time you have come, including today, your hands are like ice. I can see in your eyes that something terribly deep is bothering you. You're a nervous wreck. Would you like to talk about it? Are you having some problems in your community?"

"No, I'm really not."

I wasn't having problems with the community. I was having problems with myself, and I did feel somewhat defensive. Why should I share my problems with him? Picking this up, he said, "Well, obviously you don't want to talk about it with me. But I am concerned about you, and if I'm not the right person for you to talk to, I beg of you to find someone who is, because it's my opinion that if you don't deal with whatever it is that's upsetting you in the next couple of weeks, I don't think you'll ever be able to deal with it at all. I think something within you is going to break. You are very much on the verge of it now."

I knew what he said was true. I was no longer sleeping. When I did, I'd wake up from terrible nightmares about leaving the convent. This dream recurred during the six to eight months that I remained in Maryknoll. In my dream, I was leaving, going to the airport, saying goodbye to the nuns, and getting on the plane. Then, just as the plane started to take off, I suddenly felt that I had to return, that I had made the wrong decision and God was going to punish me. In my dream, it was too late. Every night I woke up in a cold sweat. So when the doctor said I was on the verge of a breakdown, I knew that he was right.

When I walked out, I told Sister Edith Mary, who had accompanied me, what the doctor had said. She, along with several other nuns, already knew something was going on. She started telling me what a wonderful Maryknoll nun I was, how I was one of the most ideal sisters, and that if I ever left, she would probably just give up because I represented what Maryknoll was all about. "Please don't let him affect your decision. Don't leave or pay attention to what the doctor said," she told me. And I said, "Oh, no. I don't plan to." I was still determined to stick with it.

When we got home, I went off by myself to think for a while. I still had mixed feelings, but I was beginning to feel an enormous new energy willing me to take control of my life and figure out what I wanted—needed—to do. Sister Stephanie Marie, our regional superior, had just returned from the motherhouse in New York. I knew I had to speak with her, but I wasn't sure what I was going to say. I knew I would say something though. I had reached a decision, but I couldn't express it even to myself. When she got off the plane, she told me, "Right after dinner I have important news to share with you," I said, "Wonderful, because I've got some important news to share with you too."

When I went to her office, she said, "Well, who shall go first? You said you had something important to tell me."

I said, "Well, why don't you go ahead? What did you have to tell me?"

She told me that while she was at the motherhouse, our mother general, the vicaress general, and the council had decided that I was to return to the motherhouse to be the junior formation mistress. This meant that I would become the superior of the new professed sisters and direct them in their formation as proper Maryknoll nuns. I was being offered a very important job that only an "ideal Maryknoll sister" would be asked to perform.

She said, "Mother spoke with me at great length about how pleased she has been with what you have been doing. Everyone has just been so amazed at your growth and all the things you have been able to accomplish. Sister Mercy was so thrilled by the reports that she had been getting from all corners about how you've been such a wonderful worker. They think you would be the ideal person to become a junior formation mistress."

I couldn't believe it. I said, "I don't think I will be able to go back and do that."

"Why not?"

"I'm going to leave." It was the first time I had verbalized it, even in my head.

At first, she was astounded. Then she said, "You never once mentioned to me that you were even thinking of this. But you know, I'm not surprised. I have always sensed that you were struggling with this."

She was such a sensitive, beautiful nun, and I had enormous affection for her. She had a wonderful reaction to this news. I felt terrible and was almost on the verge of tears, but she said, "I just can't believe that this is really going to happen, that you will be leaving us. But if that's what you really want, then I support you and will do everything possible to make it easier for you." We both broke down and started crying. We were overwhelmed by what had happened. I actually surprised myself with my conviction. I knew I meant it and that the decision was made for good.

I went back to my own convent and met with my psychiatrist to tell him that I had made a decision. At an earlier session, he had asked me whether this conflict between what God wanted of me and what I needed for myself had been an ongoing problem. He had suggested that perhaps I could merge these opposing interests, which was unlike Sister Ann Virginia's assertion that, "You can't think that God is such a monster. There is no way that he wants you to go through life fighting everything."

After I told him I had decided to leave, I was finally able to break through that fragmented, crazy sensation I had felt. My psychiatrist was surprised that I had decided not to stay with Maryknoll and talked about what a wonderful Maryknoll sister I was and what a shame it was to lose someone like me. He kept telling me that he wasn't sure I had made the right decision, but I had made my mind up.

I also told my superior, Marcella Marie, and she reacted fantastically. She had known what was going on with me. While I was active, nothing bothered me, when I was alone, I would cry for hours. She saw this. In fact, at one point, she had also told me that God would not ask this much of me. She really encouraged me to make the decision and was very supportive.

It was winter in Chile, probably April or May, and we were two or three months into the school year. School ended in December, and I was determined to stay until then because I knew it would be hard for them to break in a new teacher. There was no one to replace me, and I was the principal. I felt an enormous responsibility to stick around. When I told the superior, she laughed and said, "Oh God, that is so typical. You've already made your decision. I don't think you can last until the end of the school year." In her loving, supportive way, she was telling me that I had made my choice and needed to go through with it already.

Next on my agenda was to write to the mother general and tell her my decision. I outlined for her what I had been going through during my twelve years as a Maryknoll sister and what had finally brought me to make this decision. In her letter, she told me she was extremely sorry and that she never had any idea that this was happening to me. After all, I was always bright and sunny to everyone, always cheerful. She couldn't believe that I had been suffering so much underneath it all for so many years, and she was convinced that I was just exhausted from all my hard work. Perhaps I should take a leave of absence, get a good rest, take a vacation, and then come back to the order. This was a rather unusual suggestion. It wasn't something that was often offered to the nuns. Mother General practically begged me to take a leave. I replied that there was no way I would be able to do that. She wrote back that I was a person of great commitment, that Maryknoll didn't want to lose such a wonderful missionary, that it would be a shame to see me go. I replied that if this were true, then I would probably continue to be a person of great commitment after I left. You don't change your personality simply because you change your lifestyle.

I still had to let my parents know. My first letters only provided them with little hints. I suppose I was afraid of the whole Irish Catholic attitude toward going back on your promise or commitment to God. I really didn't know how my father would take it, but little by little, I warmed up to the idea of telling them. My father told me that they supported me in whatever I had to do and that they would love to have me home with them. It didn't matter; they just wanted me to be healthy and happy. This was very different from what many Irish Catholic parents did when their children made similar decisions. I had one aunt who disowned my cousin because she left the convent. My father's theology told him that my decision was wrong, but his humanity won out.

As I started the process of getting ready to leave, getting rid of things and cleaning everything out, I continued all my jobs. Before my departure date in August 1967, I had to tell the PTA, the students, and the teachers that I was leaving. Sister Marcella Marie advised me not to tell them my reason for leaving because it was too hard for the laity to accept, and they wouldn't be able to understand what I was going through. They would be scandalized, and that would make it harder for me because they might respond negatively. Instead, she told me I should just tell them that I had been reassigned to the motherhouse and that I was going back to the States. Father Shawnberg, the pastor, told me the same thing, nearly ordering me not to tell them I was leaving the convent. This had never occurred before with the Maryknoll order in Chile. The big exodus had not yet begun, so the idea of a nun leaving was still a scandalous, terrible thing. The last thing I wanted to do, he said, was to let the laity know that this was going on.

Theresa on a trail, 1967.

I gave it a great deal of thought but finally realized that I had to tell them the truth. There was no way that I could just walk out of their lives. I had become very close to some of the people and I couldn't just lie to them. So, the last week I was there, in each one of my classes, I told the students why I was going. I really loved my students and enjoyed working with them, so this was an incredibly difficult, moving experience. I broke down every time I told a class, but I had to do it. As word started leaking out to the parents, some of them came over to the school and asked whether the rumors were true and what was going to happen, who the new principal would be, and who would teach their children. The president of the PTA called a meeting and asked me to explain everything to the people. I told him I would. My superior was horrified, but said, "Go ahead and do it if you want to, but I can't stand it." She was very sentimental and said that if I started telling the parents, she would start crying, and she couldn't stand that. On our way to the meeting, she tried to make light of the situation by saying she couldn't stand me, because this decision meant that everyone had to suffer alongside me.

When I announced to the parents that I was leaving, the president of the PTA, Mr. Alarcón, came up to me and gave me a gift, a beautiful poem he had written about a canary who had everything he needed in his cage and would often sing and seem happy, but always longed for someone to open the door so he could fly away and live his own life. Mr. Alarcón said, "I think this is happening to you right now. You've been happy and you've given us a great deal. You've given us your song. We have loved you and we will miss you, but we really believe that you have to go and fly now. We will leave the cage door open for you." It was so beautiful; I couldn't believe it. Contrary to what I had been told, my meeting at the PTA was very moving, very sad, but also very beautiful. The students gave me testimonials and said their goodbyes.

My good friend Ricardo Lama presented me with a beautiful poem titled "Tu Partir . . . Theresa . . . Your Departure." I have included it here.

Partir . . . Muriendo . . .	To leave . . . dying . . .
Un pedazo de vida	A piece of life
Abadonando.	Abandoning.

Partir ... sufriendo ...
Tras sí, Amistad, cariño
Dejando.

Partir ... sonriendo ...
El camino con llanto
Regando.

Partir ... viendo ...
Corazones amigos
Sagrando.

Partir ... pensando ...
Que tu vida, nuestra vida
Se esta tristando

Partir ... sabiendo ...
Que tu alma, nuestra alma
Se esta lacerando

Partir ... sintiendo ...
El frío tembloroso del adiós
Que nos envuele ...
Danando.

Quedarse ... palpando ...
Como tu partida
Algo nos esta
Quebrajando.

Quedarse ... oyendo ...
Como al irte
Nuestra dicha se esta
Derrumbando.

Quedarse ... viendo
Como te alejas
Nos esta, gravemente
Hiriendo.

To leave ... suffering ...
Leaving behind you
Friendship, love.

To leave ... seeing ...
Watering the path
With crying.

To leave ... seeing ...
Your friends' hearts
Bleeding.

To leave ... thinking ...
That your life, our life
Is becoming sadder.

To leave ... knowing ...
That your soul, our soul
Is feeling lacerated.

To leave ... feeling ...
The tremendous coldness of
goodbye, that envelops us ...
Saddening us.

To stay ... feeling ...
That your departure
Is something
breaking us.

To stay ... hearing ...
That your leaving
Is destroying our
Happiness.

To stay ... seeing ...
That your departure
Is gravely
Wounding us.

Sonya was very affected by my decision and was heartbroken that I was leaving. We had developed quite a friendship during this time. As the date approached, though I was becoming stronger and stronger, the sadness of having to say goodbye was still there. I had gotten to love them so much. Kierkegaard has a poem about having to leap over the abyss in the midst of night that perfectly reflected the feeling I had. My decision to stay on one side of the mountain or jump to the other side became complicated by the abyss that separated the sides. Was it better to remain on one side where I knew it was safe, or to jump to the other side and see what new things were going on over there? It was also possible that I would fall in the middle of the abyss and never come out.

Once I had made my decision to leave, I had to deal with a new nightmare. I kept thinking to myself, "My God, this is terrible. What will I do? Where will I work? Who will I know? I'm thirty-two years old and there won't be anyone out there my age with my experiences." I had no idea that I was leaving right before a major exodus from the church, so it never occurred to me that I would meet male or female friends my age who had the same value system I did. I was terrified by the thought of getting a job. What would I tell the person who was interviewing me? Should I tell them I was a nun for twelve years? Where would I live? I couldn't go back to living with my parents. I was a different person. I thought, "Perhaps I'll live by myself in the Puerto Rican community in New York. I'll be alone for the rest of my life, never meet anyone or share anything with anybody. My reason for leaving will never become fulfilled because no one will be out there to receive me."

On the other hand, I knew that if I stayed with Maryknoll because of my insecurities, I would stagnate and have a nervous breakdown. At best, I would begin dying on the inside. My life would be a struggle for survival instead of a struggle to grow and develop. So while I was extremely terrified of facing life alone, I was acutely aware that I had to take this leap over the abyss. The leap was no longer theological—now it was psychological.

I decided against going back to Troy with my family and friends for fear that I would have a psychological meltdown the minute I walked through the front door. I wrote to my brother, Jackie, in California to ask if I could come and stay with him for a couple of weeks. He was older than me and had been away from home for so many years that we didn't know each other terribly well, so that seemed like the best place to have a nervous breakdown. Once this was over with and I had gotten my life together and figured out what I was going to do, I would visit the rest of my family in upstate New York, then move to New York City's Puerto Rican community.

At the time, I was seeing Sister Margaret Frances, who I would come to know as Renee, less and less because I had resigned as the chapter delegate. While waiting for an answer from my brother, I finally saw Renee and told her my decision. Word had gotten around that Renee had also decided to leave. After all we had been through together, we didn't know that we were both leaving. She said she was moving to California to live with her sister. I said, "My God, that's exactly what I'm going to do. I'm going to live with my brother in California." Then both of our siblings confirmed that we could stay with them. Renee's sister lived in Manhattan Beach and my brother lived in Torrance, so we would be just thirty minutes away from one another. We were thrilled! We planned to get together when we got out.

When the date came for me to leave, August 15, 1967, it wasn't as bad as I had imagined. I cried as I said my final farewells, but I knew that I was going to make it. There was an unbelievable strength coming back to me. At the regional house, they threw me a going-away party, and the sisters were all so wonderful. Many of them gave me very nice notes, encouraging me and telling me how much I had meant to them and how much they would miss our friendship. There wasn't a single nun who tried to hold me back or judge me for what I was doing.

Before I left, Sonya and I had gone shopping for clothes. I felt like I looked ridiculous, like an old lady. I didn't know how to fix my hair. I had funny little shoes and a dress with a rhinestone pin on it. I must have looked like I was fifty years old, which sounded ancient to me back then. The nuns were all waiting downstairs while I changed, and when I came down in my new outfit, they all thought I looked beautiful, because everything is relative.

A few of the nuns came to the airport with me, including one of my best friends, Sister Rose Carol, who would later be killed in El Salvador while working with the refugees. Though I was nervous and a little sad, I knew everything would be all right. Looking down at my hand, I exclaimed, "Oh my God, I still have my ring on!" Our Maryknoll rings were like wedding rings, signifying our marriage to God. I was obviously not allowed to take it with me. Sister Rose Carol asked me for it. "May I take it? I'm going to ask if I can keep it. This ring is very special to me, and you will always be special to me." Of course, I gave it to her.

I said goodbye and walked to the plane. I had done this in my nightmares so many times before. As soon as I got to the plane, I would realize I had made a huge mistake, but it would be too late. This time, as I walked up to the ramp, turned around, said goodbye, I was crying, but not because I had made the wrong choice. I felt as if a giant boulder had been lifted off of me. I was so positive I had done the right thing. I kept thinking, "My God, why did it take me so long? I've done it. I'm through with it. I've made the right decision and I'll never doubt myself again." I thought of all the other sisters who were struggling as I had been. Sister Patricia Mary, for instance, and a number of others. I had made the right decision, and instead of a lightning bolt of fear and regret, the whole sky opened up to reveal a beautiful rainbow.

On the plane, the stewardess came by and asked, "Would you like a drink?" It was fantastic. I hadn't had a drink in twelve years, so I said, "Yeah, that sounds great." Of course, I really didn't know how to order. I used to know, twelve years ago, but not anymore. She named a few and I said, "Yeah, that sounds wonderful," at random.

Then she asked me if I would like some cigarettes. I remember thinking this was definitely my lucky day. I said, "Yes, thank you," and I had my first drink and my first cigarette out in the open.

There was so much for me to think about, and I had a twenty-one-hour flight ahead of me to rediscover who "Theresa" was after twelve years of being "Sister Maura Killene." I could tell the two ladies next to me were gearing up for a long conversation, but I couldn't handle a conversation at that moment. I needed to be alone with "Theresa." When I was in my habit, it was understood that being a nun or a priest meant belonging to everyone. We weren't our own people; we were representing the church, and the order, and God. I never would have dreamed of ignoring someone who was trying to talk to me. But as I sat on the plane without my habit, I realized that no one knew I was a nun or anything. When the women started talking, I could finally say, "I'm sorry, but I really don't feel like talking right now. I'm just going to spend some time by myself." It may sound small, but it was so freeing and new to me. I sat there and had my drink and my cigarette and just relaxed for the next twenty-one hours, thinking, "I'm free!"

The freedom I was feeling was part religious liberation, part psychological liberation, but there was also a more trivial liberation: being able to have a drink and a cigarette and, basically, do whatever I wanted. It was a wonderful feeling, but now I had twenty-one hours of flying and stopovers to let everything sink in. Now it was time for reflection.

CHAPTER 4

LA in the Sixties: Becoming Political

I really didn't know what to expect when I got to California. My brother Jack was the sibling I knew the least, and the only member of my family who lived in California. I had only met my sister-in-law Patty once in all those years. I didn't want to go back to New York where everyone knew me because I was sure I would be a nervous wreck, and I couldn't fall apart with my whole family and all my loved ones around me all the time. I essentially came to California to have my nervous breakdown, get used to being out, and figure out what I wanted to do; then I wanted to go back to New York. But the moment I got on the plane, I thought, "No. That's not going to happen." As I left Chile I had made the decision that I was never going to live in fear again. I wrote the only poem I have written. It was based on Kierkegaard's "Leap over the Abyss." I wrote it in Spanish, but I have included an English translation here as well.

El Salto

Un salto
es como pasar
de la luz
a la obscuridad

es como pasar
por un abismo

es como pasar
desde lo conocido
hacia el desconocido

es como pasar
desde el temor
hacia la esperanza

¿a donde voy a llegar?
¿como voy a llegar?
¿Iré a llegar?
No sabemos donde
No sabemos como

Solamente Sabemos que—
Hay que saltar

¿A donde llegaremos?
A la Luz—más luz
Al conocimiento
A la experiencia
¡A la vida—!

¿Y el temor?
¿Por qué es tan potente?
¿Por qué saltar y abandonar la comodidad?
¿Que hay en el más allá?
¿Saltaré?

¡Sí Saltaré!

Aunque el salto es la cruz
El morir un poco
Llegaré a la Resurrección
¡A la luz brillante!
¡Al conocimiento real!
¡A la experiencia total!
¡A la vida plena!
Y seguiré saltando
Y seguiré muriendo para seguir viviendo
Y habrá:
una serie de llegados
una serie de "vivir de nuevo—"

Si vale la pena vivir—
Vale la pena saltar . . .
Vivir es saltar.

The Leap

A leap
is like moving
from the light
into the darkness

it is like going
through an abyss

it is like going
from the known
to the unknown

it is like ascending
from fear
to hope

where will I arrive?
how will I arrive?
Will I arrive?
We don't know where
We don't know how

We only know that—
We have to take the leap

What will we reach?
The light—more light
Knowledge
Experience
Life—!

And fear?
Why is it so strong?
Why leap and abandon comfort?
What exists in the great beyond?
Will I take the leap?

Yes, I will take the leap!

Although the leap is the cross
And dying a little—
I reach the Resurrection,
The bright light!
True knowledge!
The full experience!
Full life!
And I will continue to leap
And I will continue to die in order to live
And there will be:
a series of arrivals
a series of "living anew—"

If it's worth it to live—
It's worth it to take the leap . . .
To live is to take the leap.

Translation by Emily S. Goldman

The day I arrived in California, my sister-in-law came to pick me up with her uncle and my good friend from Chile, Renee (formerly Sister Margaret Frances). Renee and I were ecstatic that we were out and free. Renee said, "Do you want a cigarette?" Of course, I said yes, and we just smoked one after the other on the drive to my brother's house. My sister-in-law was staring at us, completely stunned to see these two ex-nuns smoking up a storm. To this day, my sister-in-law talks about the shock she was in.

Jack was wonderful, happy, and full of life, but he was also the only nonreligious person in my family, so he was a little nervous about having a nun living with him, even though I was his sister. He had told Patty and their five kids that while I was there they would have to start saying grace before meals and all kinds of other things about nuns, like how they don't smoke, and here I came in chain-smoking.

That night at dinner, my brother sat down and said, "Okay, let's say grace." I could see his kids gawking at me. Jack didn't even re-member exactly how to make the sign of the cross. I knew right away what was going on, and I said, "You know, you don't have to say grace just because I'm here."

I stayed with my brother and his family for a month or two while I was searching for a job. I had no clothes, and I was still unsure of how to dress like a normal person, but I was glad I was even able to wear regular clothes. I immediately went out to the store. I was addicted to pink, which my sister-in-law found hilarious. I got pink shorts, pink shirts, pink everything. Even shopping for clothes was all new and mind-boggling.

At the same time, I wasn't feeling very liberated yet. I had no idea how to go about looking for a job, and I was scared because I didn't know what to tell people I had been doing over the last twelve years of my life, or what my skills were. I didn't know what was out there. I knew I wanted to do something more with my life than just a job. I knew I wanted to work and live with Latin American people, but that was all I was sure about. I cared about what happened to people, but I was not really political.

Renee and I went out job hunting together in East LA. We started out riding the buses, but every time I went out by myself, I got lost. My brother took the hundred dollars Maryknoll had given me when I left to buy me a ninety-five-dollar Chevy Corvair, which was a death machine, and I didn't have any sense of geography. I still got lost every time I left the house. I went around with three-by-five cards that said "turn left here" or "turn right there."

It was the end of August. I had hoped to get a teaching job, but it was too late for that. I had a hard time with resumes because I didn't want to tell any prospective employer that I had been a nun, not because I was ashamed, but because I was worried it might influence their decision. Some people hate nuns, Catholics and non-Catholics alike, for different reasons, and you never know what people are going to think. Not everyone wants a nun in their employment. So I said, "I was in Chile working with a group. It was sort of like the Peace Corps."

I even applied for a job at the Probation Department, I was getting so desperate. Finally, I got a job from the Department of Social Services (DPSS) as a social worker in East LA. Shortly afterward, Renee also got a job in East LA with the Community Service Organization (CSO) on Whittier Boulevard. We decided to get an apartment together in East Los Angeles.

My very first day at work, my Corvair was stolen, and I had to call the police and file a report and everything. It eventually turned up in a parking lot somewhere, but that was how my first day went. When I finally did manage to get to work, my boss was wonderful. He knew my background and was very considerate of the fact that everything was new to me. When I began my casework, I was assigned to work with all Latino families, primarily Cuban and Mexican families in East LA, Compton, and Maywood.

There were enormous differences in how we were expected to treat these two groups of people. The Cubans were anti-Fidel Castro and our government loved them because they had left Cuba. When I went to their homes, they were still lamenting what Castro had done to them. They'd show me all their pictures of the beautiful homes that they had in Cuba. They all said, "Look what this horrible man did." I felt sorry for them. I didn't know that much about Castro or Cuba.

I thought they should all get to know each other, so I found a church hall and I invited all of my Cuban families to gatherings where they could have parties, help one another, and so on. I helped them build a large Cuban community.

Part of my job was visiting Cuban and Mexican American families' homes and dictating reports on what each family needed. The supervisor would then read my notes and decide what follow-up had to be done. I noticed that for the Cuban families, no matter what they asked for, we got it for them immediately. When I got requests from the Mexican American families, the response was more like, "Oh yeah. Okay. Just put it in there. We'll do it as soon as we can." It could take months or simply never happen.

The biggest part of my work ended up being with Mexican American families. We had to do a case study of everyone in the house, everyone in the family. The mothers were completely overburdened, often pregnant again with their eighth or ninth child, and many of the children were not well taken care of. They couldn't be. They didn't have the money. They didn't have the time or energy. Some of them were already on drugs. They were getting into gangs. They had all sorts of problems. One woman said to me, "My doctor told me that I am totally *gastado*." The word meant totally spent. It's like it's all gone. "There is nothing left there, of my uterus, of my health," she said. "My doctor said if I have any more children, I might not live through it."

I said, "Then you don't want to have more children, so let's go to the Planned Parenthood center and we'll get you some help."

"Oh, I can't do that. The pope just came out with a new encyclical that said birth control is absolutely a mortal sin."

Contraception—a mortal, mortal sin.

As I found out what these people were going through, I realized how many of those horrors were because of the Catholic Church. The Mexicans were a lot like the Irish I had grown up with, and they followed whatever the priest said—no matter what it was, it was absolute. If he said no contraception, then no contraception for them. I was so angry that the church would do this to people.

When I left the convent, I didn't leave the church. I still attended Mass. I kept going to different churches, thinking, "Maybe I'll find some priest who knows what his people are going through, who is trying to help them instead of putting more obligations on them and taking their money in the collections at the same time." Every Sunday I came out of church very frustrated and very angry. It seemed like the priests in East LA were all talking about bingo and about this sin and that sin. Not a word about the people's needs. The papal encyclical stated that however many children God sends you, you have to have them. I thought, "What is wrong with them? What does the pope know about what these people are going through? "

I couldn't stand to see them do this to people. Renee and I came out frustrated every week. Finally, I just decided not to go anymore. I thought, "I'm not a Catholic anymore. I don't want to be a part of this church." This was the breaking point for me both religiously and politically. I had cut myself off from anything that was exploiting the people and not helping them.

Around this time, Renee met Larry Haun, an ex-priest who had also left the church. He wasn't a Maryknoller, but he had been in Chile. They started dating right away. It was instant love, and they were married within six months. So I lost my roommate to Larry, which was kind of a shocker because I had been expecting Renee and me to go out and hit the town together.

That was, however, the beginning of my political education. Larry Haun was very political, and he was my mentor for a while. He took us to farm worker demonstrations and to the napalm factory in Torrance to protest the war. It seemed like we were constantly going to demonstrations. I went to everything because I was eager to learn more about what I wanted to get involved in. I was learning more about the difference between charity and justice and about what needed to be done. We needed to do a lot more than just give small handouts to people. It was a slow learning curve for me, but I was learning by being there.

I shouldn't have been surprised that Renee had started dating Larry. I was ready to date about two days after I got out. It just took a while. This was the sixties, so there weren't as many thirty-two-year olds still on the market, and certainly no one that I knew who matched my values. I had no interest in going to a singles bar or anything like that. I just knew if I was going to meet anyone, I would meet him doing what I do. My first date was with a guy who interviewed me for a job with the probation department. It was horrible. It took a couple of months after Renee and Larry got together before I met Terry Grace. Terry had been a Christian brother, but he was only in for a very short time, and he had been out quite a long time. He was more a man of the world by then. We started going out.

With society's upheaval in the 1960s, religious communities began redefining themselves, within and without, as thousands of individuals left for personal reasons. Many of the nuns and priests who'd left their convents and parishes for secular life during this convulsing period in the Catholic Church didn't abandon their calling along with their vows and clerical habits. Their abandonment elicited tremors throughout society as they morphed into lay communities across the world and continued to assist and lend their emotional, spiritual, and physical support to the downtrodden of the world.

When I left, I still felt like I was one of the pioneers. Now, little by little, we were getting word that nuns, priests, and everybody were coming out. Somehow they began finding us. Terry had a bright idea. He had heard about a house in Alhambra that was for lease. Terry said, "Why don't we get this house and turn it into a community house? That way the nuns and priests coming out will have a some-where to go, like a halfway house." So we did. We leased the house.

The people who leased it to us were Catholics, so of course they asked, "Are you married?"

"We will be by the time we move in," we lied through our teeth. We were nowhere near marriage.

They leased the house to us for a year.

Most of the former religious understood very little about transitioning from a religious environment to a secular one and discovered a world they'd been out of touch with for several years, some for a lifetime. They knew that for the sake of their own sanity, they had to take on this challenge and step into a fast-paced and changing global arena. Many had no place to call home or no way to find shelters to accommodate them. Once they'd left their convent or seminary, many had no money, no car, very few of life's necessities. We didn't need to worry about how to reach out to ex-clergy. Word quickly spread through the ex-clergy grapevine about the Alhambra House. Former clergy who found themselves at a crossroads, who didn't know whether to stay or go, discovered us, found their way to our door when their needs presented themselves.

It seemed like word got out overnight about our place, and the house filled up quickly. A number of other nuns and priests who had left came there. Phyllis Menard, who became a close friend, had been a nun in Peru. She was a nurse and had been thrown out for teaching about birth control. That wasn't only against the teachings of the Catholic Church, but her order nearly flipped when they found out. They sent her to the United States. She had nowhere to go, but someone in Peru told her about our Alhambra House. I thought it was unbelievable that someone had heard about our house way out in Peru. She came to LA to find the Alhambra House. One night, around midnight, her aunt threw her out for not going to Mass with her. We gave her a room and taught her the ways of the world in one quick and easy lesson.

It was very interesting, and a little funny, to watch the ex-clergy adapt to the world. My good friend Cam French, who lived with us at Alhambra House as a young single mother, remarked, "It was like watching them go from zero to a thousand every time they approached a new challenge and conquered it. In the space of a few months, I watched them make up those lost years socially, politically, and sexually. They weren't going to leave any stone unturned. These women may not have known an eyebrow pencil from a Crayola or a stiletto from a kitten heel, and this is where I was at an advantage. This was my role. To assist them in presenting themselves to the workplace. To advise on dress, hair, and makeup. "

For the most part, the Alhambra House functioned like a well-oiled, though small, community. Everyone held a job. Their paychecks went for rent and food, helping other ex-clergy, and each person's individual needs, such as toiletries, gas, insurance, etc. I drew up house rules, a monthly list of house-cleaning assignments meted out to each of us, schedules for grocery shopping (we bought food collectively), and cooking. We held a weekly meeting for discussions regarding all matters pertaining to the house, suggestions for improvement, and the inevitable complaints. Everything had to be voted on. Even though we were initially clumsy with it, no one's vote was more important than anyone else's vote. We had consensus. We were a collective. If you had two of something and someone needed it, you would share it. It gave birth to the first ideas of collective living.

I'm sure our neighbors wondered about us, all these thirty-year-olds coming and going so frequently. We all had our little VW bugs and were running in and out all the time, going off to our various jobs.

I knew I didn't want to continue as a social worker, so I started to apply for teaching jobs. In the meantime, there were priests and nuns leaving in a mass exodus. They formed a group—kind of a corporate group—called "Bearings for Reestablishment," as in "ball bearings." It was a ridiculous name, but it brought all these nuns and priests together, giving us classes, teaching us to write resumes and translate what we did into secular language. You had to pay a fee for it, but

I went to these classes anyway and, shortly after, got a job teaching English as a Second Language at the Mexican American Opportunity Foundation in East LA.

I started going to the Catholic Peace Association, where I met a lot of people who were like me, and we started to gravitate toward politics. Renee's husband, Larry Haun, had started the politicization by taking us to all those demonstrations. Anywhere there was a demonstration, Larry knew about it.

That's when I became aware of how differently people treated me without a habit on. I dressed like everybody else, in the short skirts that were fashionable at the time, and I'd be running around the demonstrations, dodging the police, who were pushing and pulling us, and being screamed at by people calling us communists. When I was wearing my habit, it was all, "Oh, Madre, you're so respectful. You're such a good person," and now, all of a sudden, I was being treated like the scum of the earth.

About this time I met Jim Donaldson, a Methodist minister who was an absolutely brilliant guy. He came up with the idea of starting something called the "Urban Plunge." Renee, Larry, and I, and all of us who had left the church, were ready to jump right in, as we were with anything that had to do with social action.

Once a month, we all went to a church that let us use their hall all Friday night. We had a whole program about Martin Luther King, Jr. and Kennedy, Cesar Chavez, you know, all the people that should be inspiring us to change our country. It was total political activism time. The program lasted for a couple of hours, and then we carried on listening to music and dancing until the wee hours of the morning. We slept on the floor in sleeping bags. We often spent the rest of the night talking.

The next day, groups like the Black Panthers and the Brown Berets would come give talks about what was happening in their communities. In the afternoon, we went out into the community, maybe to Black Panther or Brown Beret headquarters to see them in their environment.

Saturday night, we went to Skid Row to see how the people lived. We went into the tattoo shops and walked around with all the people that were drunk. We tried to talk to them. There were porn shops all around.

We went to gay and lesbian bars. We went in, sat down and had a drink, but we were so unused to that kind of environment that we didn't know what to expect. I was very naïve, but that quickly disappeared because every other person I met was gay. I realized then that we were all really in the same place.

Finally, we went back to our church. We had workshops on how to address the problems of the inner city and how to get more upper and middle-class people interested. It was extremely exciting.

I began to notice that Jim Donaldson was a bit like a cult guru. He was extremely charismatic and intelligent, and I think I was one of the first ones to realize that this guy was trying to control us. He began trying to manipulate us sexually, telling us that we should all be bisexual, and that if you're not bisexual you're not really living. Married couples shouldn't just be stuck with each other, he said, they needed to move around. The whole time, he was making advances on all the members of the group, trying to make out with everyone. I would have no part of that at all. I lost all my respect for him. Eventually, he left, and the last thing I heard of him was that he was in Mexico doing God knows what.

I stayed in the group because I felt we were doing effective work. We were bringing middle-class people in to see things they had never seen. It was very similar to what we did in Chile, bringing the rich kids up to the mountains. The people who participated in Urban Plunge listened to groups like the Black Panthers and the Brown Berets. We were bringing these rich families, most of whom were middle and upper-class whites, to Skid Row, to gay and lesbian bars. They found out that we're all brothers and sisters.

It was about this time that I met Blase. Like everyone else, I had already heard about Blase. He had been a Maryknoll priest in Guatemala where the CIA had helped overthrow the democratically elected government in 1954, largely to advance the interests of the United Fruit Company. The result was a bloody civil war that lasted until the 1990s.

At the same time, the liberalization of the church following Vatican II had led to the emergence of liberation theology in Latin America. In 1967, Blase wrote in his journal, "I do not intend to become accustomed to the poverty and destitution of these poor people. I do not intend to become accustomed to their sickness, ignorance, to the constant injustices they receive. I do intend to do whatever I can to change these evils." Blase set out to do what he could to change the conditions faced by the people of Guatemala. The local people called him a "guerilla for peace."

Blase standing in a classroom, 1967.

In early 1968, the Guatemalan government accused nuns and priests associated with the Maryknoll order of fomenting a communist revolution in the country. Blase was ordered to leave Guatemala. Maryknoll ordered him to a parish in Hawaii and placed him under a gag order. Instead, Blase returned to his family's home in Los Angeles. He went to the *Washington Post* and released information proving that the US was militarily engaged with death squads in Guatemala and was using napalm on the indigenous people.

It would have been hard not to have heard of Blase.

I was still dating Terry Grace at the time. Larry Haun had known Blase when he was a priest, and he always said, "Theresa, I love Terry. I think he's really nice, but he's just not your caliber. You have to meet Blase." Blase was speaking all over the country, so when he came to town for a speaking engagement, we all went.

There wasn't really a spark at first. Blase was still too much of a priest. He still often wore his collar, and he hadn't really accepted that they had thrown him out. He treated me like a priest would, and I remember chatting with him one night at a Black Panther fundraiser and thinking, "He's a priest, no question." I didn't think he was even an option. But we kept running into each other.

Our lease at the Alhambra House was about to expire, so we had to close the house. The night we closed it, we threw a big party. Blase came to that party, and that's when we first really connected. It evolved slowly. We began dating in June 1969. It was like building a friendship first, and then we fell in love.

Phyllis Menard, Cam, a single mother who had lived with us on Alhambra, and I moved to a house in Monterey Park. Blase lived nearby in Los Feliz. We were both involved with a group called *Católicos por la Raza.*

The group was organized because the archbishop, Cardinal McIntyre, decided to build St. Basil's Church (we called it St. Basil's Cathedral) in the middle of all the horrors and poverty downtown. It was a four-million-dollar project, which in 1969 seemed monumental to us. Many of the poor people living in that area were Latinos who went to their church every week and donated their meager resources. Instead of giving them something back, the church used it for something that would practically exclude them. The Chicano movement decided to unite around that and called the group *Católicos por la Raza*. We joined the group and went to meetings in East Los Angeles, attended demonstrations, and protested that the money should go toward the betterment of the people instead of the construction of this edifice that would not serve anybody. McIntyre was angry because there were a lot of ex-nuns and ex-priests in the group. He came out with a lot of proclamations that said we were all terrible people and that no one should listen to us, that the church was going to be a tribute to God. So they went ahead and built the cathedral.

While we were part of *Católicos por la Raza*, Blase was teaching at UCLA. We had been working a lot with the Black Panthers, and December 1969 was a very tense time for them. On December 4, the FBI and Chicago Police Department had attacked the Chicago apartment of a Panther leader, killing four Panthers. Four days later, Blase, who was the Panther minister of religion, got a phone call at 5:00 a.m. The LAPD was storming Black Panther headquarters in South Central.

The caller said, "Blase, we need you. There going to be a shootout at the Black Panther headquarters. We're afraid they're going to throw grenades. They're ready to roll and they're going to kill everybody. Can you come down here and do something? Wear your collar."

I wasn't there. Blase was at his own apartment. He put on his collar and his priest clothes and he went down to the Black Panther headquarters. When he got there, the media had already arrived.

Blase went up to an Irish police captain, who was as Catholic as he could be. Blase said, "Hi, I'm Father Bonpane. What's going on?"

"They won't come out, and we're going to go after them."

Blase said, "Let's see if we can get them to surrender and come out."

The cop said, "No, we're going in shooting. They've been in there long enough. We've got to do this."

Blase tried to reason with him. "Look, why don't we just give them a chance. Some already have white handkerchiefs at the window."

The media was there, recording the whole thing. Fortunately, the captain listened. Eventually, the Panthers came out and surrendered, were arrested, and went to trial.

That night on television, the newscaster said, "Father Blase Bonpane, UCLA professor . . ." The minute I saw it, I said, "Well, Blase, there goes your job at UCLA."

We didn't worry about it at the time. We were busy with *Católicos por la Raza.* The group had decided to have a demonstration at St. Basil's Cathedral on Christmas Eve 1969—a midnight Mass.

Blase and several others were asked to say part of the Mass.

Blase at a demonstration, 1969.

Several hundred of us showed up that night, demonstrating with our signs as Blase started the services. In the meantime, wealthy people from outside the neighborhood were entering the church in their furs and rhinestones. Anybody who wasn't elegantly dressed was questioned by the ushers before they were admitted to make sure they weren't demonstrators. Three ex-nuns in our group borrowed clothes and dressed up. They got in. The Mass inside the church was televised so the cardinal could watch and point out people who shouldn't have been there. When they got to the part of the gospel where Joseph and Mary, looking for a place for the baby Jesus to be born, were told there was no room at the inn, our group on the inside started yelling out in the church: "There's no room at the inn tonight because the poor people are again put outside, just like Joseph and Mary were put outside." It was a perfect connection because, like Mary and Joseph, the poor people were locked outside. The ex-nuns inside began to yell, "Let the poor people in!" We could hear them outside, and everybody outside began to yell, "Let the poor people in!" Some of our outside troops were trying to get in. Our people inside were immediately pulled out by the ushers, who we later discovered were policemen in plainclothes. They had batons ready to go. Anybody who was inside or who tried to get inside the church was immediately arrested.

Outside, everybody within four blocks of the church got a warning. The cops drove up and told us, "If you don't disperse in three minutes, you'll be arrested." They didn't wait three minutes. They appeared out of nowhere, swinging their batons, hitting everybody, throwing them, arresting them, and indiscriminately beating them.

There were a lot of cameras there from the press—some of our group had cameras as well—so we had a lot of evidence of what happened. The people who were inside the church were arrested and brought to trial. For that action of yelling out in the church, they got ninety days. The same day, a doctor who killed his wife got ninety days in a rehabilitation psychiatric hospital—the same ninety days our people were sentenced.

Blase and I were not arrested that night. We thought we were lucky. In the days following, many in our group got subpoenas to appear in court. They were told the police had their pictures. We were the only ones who didn't get a subpoena. This was very strange considering how well-known Blase was. Ultimately, we learned that Evelle Younger, the district attorney, lived next door to Blase's father, Judge Blase Bonpane. We couldn't be sure, but it seemed like they had a hit list and somebody said ahead of time, "Let's not get Blase, his father's a judge."

During the *Católicos por la Raza* campaign, Blase and I spent a lot of time together. After protests, we often went over to Olvera Street for a drink. On December 9, as we were walking through the little shops, I spotted some friendship rings. I hardly ever wore rings, but I wanted one. I found one for about $4.95 and said, "I'll buy this one."

Instead, Blase offered to buy it for me.

"Okay, then I'll buy one for you too," I responded, and we found him a ring for about the same price.

At the chapel on Olvera Street, there was a wedding going on.

Blase said, "Now that we've got rings, maybe we should get married."

Of course, I agreed.

First, we notified his family that we planned to get married on January 1. We never sent out formal invitations or made any phone calls. Instead, at demonsrations between December 9 and January 1, we handed out fliers to our personal friends that said we would be married on January 1 and included the address. Some of those people invited other people, and we said that was fine. We were so out of it, we hardly did anything in preparation. We didn't even realize that we should be preparing. Blase's eighty-year-old mother got the caterers for us. Two days before the wedding, I went with a couple of friends to buy a dress. We just pulled together this little ceremony.

On January 1, 1970, we got married at his parents' beautiful house. We decided to marry ourselves. There were so many priests and ex-priests in the audience that we figured we were taken care of, even if we didn't have a formal priest.

The wedding was absolutely wonderful. Everybody who was there was in the movement, and we had asked that instead of bringing gifts, everyone should bring a reading or a thought or a poem to share at the ceremony. Everything people read was revolutionary; it was "revolution this," and "revolution that," and, "I hope you have a very revolutionary baby." Blase's parents were dumbstruck, and Blase's father had a fit when we tried to pass around a chalice full of wine; he didn't want all those germs going around in his house.

After the wedding, one of Blase's cousins, Vincent Bonpane, wrote a letter to Blase's father which said, "I have never been so ashamed in my life to have the name Bonpane as I was at that wedding." He couldn't stand the talk about the revolution and the Black Panthers who, he believed, were there.

In fact, we hadn't gotten around to inviting the Panthers because we simply hadn't seen them in the weeks immediately before the wedding, so they didn't get the flier. Blase's cousin Vincent said, "When they started singing the Black Panther hymn, I gave up." We thought, "Black Panther hymn? What is he talking about?" So we thought about all the songs we sang, and one of them was "Born Free," and he must have thought that was their hymn.

The only family I had at the wedding were my California relatives: my brother Jackie, his wife Patty, their five kids, and Jackie's sister-in-law. The rest were Bonpanes. Blase's sister, a nun, was sent by her mother general in case her parents needed moral support to deal with Blase getting married. In fact, Blase's parents were thrilled. They had always wanted him to get married; they hadn't wanted him to become a priest. Maybe Blase's father already had an inkling of what was ahead, but he hoped that when we got married, we would live a normal life. As time went on, Blase's father became very angry at me for not helping Blase settle down.

Blase and Theresa cutting their wedding cake, 1970.

We went on a three-day honeymoon to Palm Springs. When we came back, I returned to the Mexican American Opportunity Foundation, where I was working, and Blase went back to UCLA. When he got there, the parking lot attendant said, "You don't have a parking place here anymore."

"Why not?" Blase asked.

"Because you don't work here anymore. I got a notice here that somebody else has that parking slot."

Blase said, "I do work here. I was here a couple of weeks ago. I'm working here."

"No, you're not."

Blase had to go investigate to find out that he'd been fired. Of course, we knew it was because his name had been on television after the Black Panther shootout. Ronald Reagan, who was governor of California at the time, had already identified him as one of the bad guys because he knew Angela Davis.

I had married a successful UCLA professor, and three days later, he was out of a job.

Blase just couldn't find another job. He was totally blacklisted. We knew exactly what was happening. During our first year, he had thirteen interviews. At every one, he was told, "You're a fantastic candidate, a perfect fit. We are going to hire you." And after each interview, he got a notice that the position or the program had been canceled and they couldn't hire him after all. We later got documentation which proved that he was being blacklisted.

Blase and Theresa listening to speeches at their wedding, 1970.

At the time, we were working for the Berrigan Defense Committee and the Chicano Moratorium to protest the Vietnam War. We were constantly involved in many different political things.

Since he couldn't get a job, Blase went on unemployment. While he was on unemployment, he decided to run for Congress. None of us knew anything about campaigns. We hadn't even been around any campaigns, let alone run one. Blase thought it would be a good forum for his politics, and he thought he might win. Blase got everything started, but he had no campaign manager, so his best friend and former Maryknoller Bob Menard took on that role. Of course, with no experience running for office or campaigning in general, for that matter, Blase lost the election, but we learned a lot from the whole experience.

In May of 1970 the people who had been subpoenaed for our Christmas Eve St. Basil's demonstration had to go to court. Oscar Acosta, who was the lawyer for some of our cases, asked Blase to come as an expert witness. Acosta asked Blase to wear his collar so he could establish that there were priests inside the church as well as outside. Blase said, "Fine, I'm still a Catholic priest. I can do that." On the stand, Blase wore his collar and Acosta questioned him to establish his background as a priest.

When the prosecutor got up for his cross-examination, he said, "I don't think I'm supposed to call you 'Father Bonpane.'"

Blase said, "Okay, that's fine."

"You claim to be a priest."

"I am a priest," Blase replied.

The prosecutor asked, "What's that ring on your finger?"

"That's my wedding band."

"Catholic priests can't be married."

Blase quoted things from the scriptures, refuting this. "A priest is a priest forever, according to the order of Melchizedek," he said, along with some other quotes.

The prosecutor said, "I know that celibacy is required in the Catholic church, and if you're married, I think you're no longer celibate."

The whole audience started laughing. The judge banged his gavel and said, "Celibacy is not the issue of the court. This is not a court to decide on celibacy."

Everybody was hysterical. The judge banged on his gavel and said, "If you start laughing one more time, I'll have the whole courtroom cleared." And eventually, the prosecutor moved on to what actually happened that night.

In addition to Blase, Acosta called several other witnesses. He asked one of them, "You were there that night. Were you allowed to go into the Catholic Church? Isn't the Catholic Church supposed to be a 'universal church'? Isn't that what the word 'Catholic' means?'"

"Yes, it is," the witness said.

"But they wouldn't let you in," Acosta questioned.

"No they didn't, they pushed me away. In fact, the police, who were dressed as ushers, practically knocked me down."

Acosta asked, "And these were Christians?"

The whole courtroom became hysterical again. The judge was having a difficult time trying to maintain order.

That was the day they decided that the three ex-nuns who had dressed up in fancy clothes and gotten inside the church were guilty. Some of the outside demonstrators were arrested for assault and battery and other things that the police had fabricated.

That summer, after Blase lost the election, we were both working summer jobs in a poverty program in East LA. I was the office manager, teaching the young women how to run an office, and Blase was the field representative. I was about six months pregnant with our daughter Colleen.

One day when Blase was out in the field, two guys all dressed up in suits came into the office. All of the kids in the office went running, saying, "It's the cops, it's the FBI." Sure enough, one of the men came over and showed his FBI badge and said, "We're looking for Blase Bonpane."

I told somebody to go and tell Blase to come in.

When he got there one of the guys said, "We have some questions for you."

They were looking for Angela Davis. They told us they had reason to believe Blase could help find her. Blase said, "What makes you think I could find Angela Davis?"

"We have her little black book and your name is in it."

They were, of course, trying to intimidate us. They knew we weren't close enough to her to know where she was, but they wanted to send a message. All the kids were afraid of the FBI and were surprised that it was us they wanted.

In August, the Chicano Moratorium had a huge demonstration against the war in Vietnam. People marched from Whittier Boulevard in East LA to Laguna Park. Everyone was congregating, the stage was set up, and there was a band playing. There were thousands of people there. We were standing in a little circle with some friends we had just met, waiting for things to start happening. I saw some young kids playing with beer cans near the liquor store we were gathered next to. They were throwing the cans around, some hitting the side of the building. The owner had just come out, and I said, "Blase, this is not a good day for them to start aggravating the owner of that liquor store. He could call the cops, and that would not be good for us." No sooner had the words left my mouth than I saw a tidal wave of police arrive. We were in the park and the police were all running, gas masks already on, helmets on, with their bullets and guns, totally prepared for war. We saw it start.

Later the police said, "There was a big ruckus and some of the demonstrators were doing some awful things."

But I was there, and I saw exactly what had happened: nothing. We were just getting ready for the rally to start. The speakers hadn't even spoken yet. The police were looking for an excuse to come in and ruin the whole thing. They descended on us like a wave. I was four months pregnant. Without so much as a warning, they started throwing tear gas at the crowd. It seemed like the tear gas was coming from everywhere, and they already had their masks on. Tear gas is awful stuff, bad for everybody, especially for the baby I was carrying. So we ran. We had never run so fast in our lives. We left our car wherever we had parked it. Our friends, the Menards, were living in East Los Angeles, so we ran the six or eight blocks from the park to their house. By this time, the entire East Los Angeles area was a war zone. There were police helicopters and cars everywhere. It was like they had prepared for this. Everybody was running, there was tear gas everywhere. It was unbelievable. That's the day, of course, that Ruben Salazar, a reporter for the *LA Times*, was killed a couple of blocks away from where we were. We had to stay at the Menards's until the next morning.

We were living in an apartment on Corinth Street at the time. This was around the time of the Sharon Tate murder, and the house was being sublet by Ron Hughes, who was one of Charles Manson's lawyers.

Ron Hughes was living in the garage while we lived in the house. We saw a lot of strange people coming and going. We knew that there were a lot of drugs back there.

One day Ron Hughes saw me coming home with bags of groceries and asked, "Where do you get your groceries?"

"Ralph's."

He said, "Why don't you come out with the family? We find some really good stuff." They were dumpster diving.

"What family?"

"You know, 'the family.'" He was talking about the Charles Manson Family.

I said, "Oh no. I think we're okay for right now. We'll keep going to Ralph's."

As time went on we knew that things were looking fishier out in the back. One night at about four thirty or five o'clock in the morning, we heard a loud noise outside our bedroom. It was clearly somebody right outside our window. I couldn't help thinking about Sharon Tate. We called the police. By the time they arrived, it was beginning to get light. They went out back to the garage and looked around the property, but they said they didn't see anything.

When they left, Ron Hughes came over and said, "Don't you ever do that again. You'll be sorry. We had to drop everything we had down the toilet, and we don't do that easily." It was really a threat. We thought, "Oh great, now Charlie Manson and his lawyer are out to get us." We couldn't wait to move.

While we were finishing up with the jobs in East LA, we got word that a job Blase had applied for in Santa Paula wanted to interview him. They had a thirty-six-person board because it was a Title VII program, so the interview was like a whole community gathering. After the interview, it was unanimous, everybody wanted Blase Bonpane. They hired him and we found a home in Santa Paula.

The weekend before we moved in, Blase got a call from the United Farm Workers. One of their workers had been killed in the fields and they wanted to have a memorial. They asked Blase to come to say the memorial Mass in Oxnard, which was where all the growers lived. Blase got up at 5:00 a.m. to go to the memorial. I said, "I have a feeling that this might affect your job."

He said, "I know," but he did it anyway.

On Sunday we moved to Santa Paula. When we went out the door on Monday to meet our new neighbors, the newspaper was on our porch. The headline was "Communist Bonpane in Santa Paula." The article said that we were communists and that Blase had been thrown out of Guatemala for subversive activity.

Blase went off to work. He had been there a couple of times and they loved him. They couldn't wait to get him because he spoke Spanish, and they planned for him to be the liaison between the Latin American Community and the Anglo community. They were just ecstatic about his role. When he got to work the morning the article came out, they told him he was not allowed to go out in the field until they got this straightened out.

In Santa Paula, only five or six people usually came to school board meetings. At the first meeting after we moved, five hundred people who wanted to fire Blase Bonpane showed up.

The paper continued to write about us being communists.

We had to go to all the board meetings where the board discussed firing Blase. One of the board members said, "Mrs. Bonpane is pregnant and their baby is going to be born in December. I don't think we can throw them out on the street."

A woman who used to harass us every time we went in or out of a board meeting jumped up and said, "We don't want a communist baby born here!" Everybody clapped for her. Everybody was on her side. They all wanted us out.

The board finally decided they had to honor Blase's contract, but he would not be allowed to go out into the community and do his job. They paid him and made him come to the office every day, but he had nothing to do. He had to sit there every day for eight hours doing nothing. It was the only time I ever saw Blase cry or be depressed. He loves to work and they wouldn't let him do community work of any kind. He just had to sit there.

When I went to the grocery store or the cleaners or the library, as soon as I'd sign a check or something, they'd say, "Bonpane. Are you married to Blase Bonpane?" When I said yes, they said, "I want you to know that I signed the petition to get you out of town. We don't want your kind of people here." We only had three friends in the Anglo community, but there were some people in the Latino community who understood that we were there to help them.

People followed Blase any place he went. There was a woman we called "The Thrifty Store Lady" who followed him everywhere with a tape recorder. He was getting some speaking engagements at the Unitarian Church and places like that, and she just followed him around, recording him. That horrible congressman Charles Teague gave out portfolios about Blase's subversive history to people in the community to make sure everyone knew about him.

We were still running the Berrigan Defense Committee in LA

at the time, so we just focused more and more on our political work there.

No one really spoke to us except to tell us they had signed the petition to get us out of town. We'd come home to hate notes in our mailbox.

Colleen was born in LA. At the hospital, we were waiting for a natural birth, but after twenty-four hours of labor, the doctor said, "We'll have to do a Cesarean." Since we didn't know if it was going to be a boy or a girl, we were thinking Blase or Martin, after my father, for a boy. If it was a girl, her name would be Colleen. When we went into the operating room, I decided not to have any drugs at all, just a spinal block. Meanwhile, the doctors were all talking about yachts and other frivolous things. I couldn't believe it. Here I was, part of history, about to have this baby, and they were talking about yachts. Then, there she was: a girl. Colleen.

I can remember when I first saw Colleen, it was like she was already saying, "Well, what's happening? Let's do something, let's get started right now." She was wide awake and ready to get on with life, and she's been that way ever since.

I think babies teach us a great deal, and we certainly learned a lot of new things from our daughter. We really tried to be in communication with her, and we realized how wonderfully bright she was, how she caught on to everything. It was a beautiful experience after all those years in religious life to have our own child. It was just the most wonderful thing imaginable.

When we came back to Santa Paula, we got out of the car, and the lady who lived across the street waved to us. We were shocked. We waved back. As we were going inside, the phone rang. I rushed inside to answer it. When I said hello, the caller said, "Mrs. Bonpane, I'm your neighbor across the street."

I said, "Was that you who waved to us?"

"Yes."

"That was so nice of you."

She started crying and said, "I knew you were having a baby, so I mentioned to some people in the neighborhood that maybe we could do a shower to welcome the baby. They said, 'If you ever go near that house or that baby or that family, you'll be sorry. Your house will be burned down.'"

I said, "You won't have to worry. We'll be out of here in June."

"Oh no," she said, "I'm already making plans. I can't live in a community like this."

Blase's father, a judge, forced the newspaper to issue a retraction. We're sorry. We said some things we probably shouldn't have said. That kind of retraction. Of course, it meant nothing to the people in the community.

Eventually, we learned that Congressman Charles Teague had circulated Blase's dossier from the House Un-American Activities Committee and his FBI file throughout the entire community. This was what was inciting all of the hatred. We also found that the House Un-American Activities Committee document had been following us throughout all of Blase's job pursuits. Teague gave out this document to any person who went to his office or anyone he felt could be a fighter against us. We were, of course, very nervous about the death threats and people following us.

One day, after Blase went off to work, I was home with Colleen when the front doorbell rang. There were two men at the door. I didn't open it, but pulled the curtain and said, "Who is it?"

They showed their badge and said, "FBI."

I opened the door, thinking it was related to all of the stuff with Blase, and said, "My husband's at work and I'm not going to invite you in. You'll have to go see him at work or something."

They said, "No, this is about an unrelated issue. We're here about the case of Ron Hughes, Charles Manson's lawyer. He was killed up in the mountains. We understand that you're a friend of his."

I called Blase and said, "You better come home. The FBI is here." We explained everything.

As the year in Santa Paula was ending, we were constantly running down to LA to organize the Berrigan Defense Committee to defend Daniel and Phillip Berrigan, the antiwar priests. We found out one of our chief helpers and workers was an FBI agent himself. He was a provocateur who frequently said, "Let's burn the flag."

Many years later, Blase got the Freedom of Information material and the ACLU found out that the FBI had been following Blase around and ruining his chances for all those jobs.

It was an incredible year. It was difficult and horrible in many ways, but I had decided one thing when I left Chile: I was never going to live in fear again. It was fear that had kept me in the convent for twelve years, and I wouldn't let fear control me ever again. When I went to South Central to the Black Panther meetings, people would say, "You can't go to South Central!" When I moved to East LA, my brother said, "Theresa, East LA? Living in East LA?" Everybody thought everything was frightening. I didn't think anything was frightening.

CHAPTER 5

Joining the Farm Workers

Cesar Chavez's people at the United Farm Workers (UFW) knew that Blase had said the Mass for the farmworker that was killed the weekend before we moved to Santa Paula, but they didn't know much about what had been happening to us after that. It got out in the papers that Blase had said Mass at the farmworker's funeral, people began to say we were in Santa Paula to organize the farmworkers, and we got a call from Chris Hartmire, the Farm Workers' Minister of Religion, one of their top people and an incredible guy. He didn't allude to everything else that was going on.

He said that Cesar wanted to start a university for the farmworkers and that he wanted us to come up to the UFW compound, near Tehachapi, where Cesar had bought an old TB hospital and turned it into headquarters. He called the compound La Paz.

We thought about it a lot. Blase was really excited about it. For one thing, he was on so many blacklists that it wasn't that easy for him to get a job anymore. I was a little less enthusiastic about it because it meant moving up to Tehachapi, to the mountains, and I'm a city person through and through. And after the way we had been treated in Santa Paula, I was really missing friendships, community, and regular neighborhood activities. I wanted to move to Echo Park where my friends lived and do food co-ops and child co-ops and book club meetings and all of those lovely things I hadn't gotten to do in the last year. But we went over the whole Farm Workers proposal, and I knew it was a good cause. I thought it would be a good thing for us to do. I was apprehensive, but we were interested in the cause and wanted to do something worthwhile, so we told Chris Hartmire we would do it.

Theresa's AFL/CIO Farm Worker ID Card, 1972.

LeRoy Chatfield, one of Cesar's top men, conducted a final interview for the job and explained a lot to us. He said, "I want you to know, Blase, as a priest or an ex-priest, that a lot of the ex-priests have problems with Cesar, because the priests are used to being Mr. Number One and Mr. Important, and in the union, it all goes to Cesar."

Blase said, "That's not a problem at all."

Blase was getting paid in Santa Paula through June, so we stayed there until his contract ran out. Then we really had no place to live until we were supposed to go to La Paz in September. We spent the rest of the summer with our baby daughter minding people's houses while they were on vacation.

When we arrived at La Paz in September of 1971, we were told there would be a trailer for us to live in. When we got out there with all of our furniture and our things and a nine-month-old Colleen, we found that the trailer had not arrived yet.

They told us there was a little house down by the railroad station in Keene, about twenty-five miles from the compound, that we could use temporarily until the trailer came. The house was a dump, a shack, a hovel—I don't know what else to call it. It looked like it started out as a railroad car with another little railroad car added on as a bedroom, and then someone kind of rigged up some things so there was something like a kitchen, but not quite, and something like a bathroom. It was just pieces of things cobbled together, and it was filthy dirty. There was a big yard that belonged to someone else that was full of pigs that smelled the place up. It was horrible, absolutely horrible. But we were so filled with zeal that we thought, "This is how the farmworkers live, and if the farmworkers have to live like this, I guess we're going to have to live like this for a while." So we started cleaning it up.

After we moved in, we found out there were rats. Colleen had to sleep in bed with us. We never could trust that she would be safe if we put her in the crib. We stayed there, living like that, for three or four months until the trailer came.

It was my belief that they could have made things a little easier for a family coming in. Little by little, we began to understand that was not the spirit of the thing. Cesar wanted us to really understand how the farmworkers lived; to leave our privilege behind and experience their conditions. We just tried to roll with it.

We were supposed to be there to start a university for the farmworkers, teaching English or the history of the labor movement, beneficial information that could also help them get more out of life. That was immediately put aside because there was always an emergency, something higher priority. For a while, we were assigned to go into the fields to try to get the growers to pay the farmworkers. We would live in a little RV. We said we would do it. We wanted to do the work.

Dolores Huerta, the cofounder of the UFW, said, "I'm so glad we are getting one of those RVs for you, because maybe now we can get some for the rest of us." Then the plan to send us out into the fields fell through.

Instead, they sent us out in October on a major campaign for

"No on 22." Proposition 22 was an initiative backed by the growers which would have undermined the Farm Workers' existing contracts and stripped them of the right to strike, picket, and boycott. We have a picture of little Colleen holding a "No on 22" bumper sticker.

I can't believe how crazy we were. Yet again, we had no place to stay; we just headed down to the San Fernando Valley to start organizing the churches, get speaking engagements, and let everybody know what this "No on 22" campaign was about.

When we got to the Bell/Compton area of LA, we went to a phone booth on the street and started calling churches. We said we were like Mary and Joseph with our little baby, and there was no room at the inn. We told them we were from the Farm Workers and asked if there was a chance that they had a place for us to stay while we conducted the campaign. A minister in Bell said, "I know about the Farm Workers and what you're trying to do. You can stay with our family." So we did.

Theresa and Blase with Cesar Chavez, 1974.

Marshall Ganz, Jessica Gouvea, and LeRoy Chatfield, some of Cesar's best organizers, were running the campaign. They were top organizers, unbelievably brilliant, and very, very hard to work for. They were so exacting. Everything I know about organizing, I learned from them.

LeRoy was the coordinator for LA. He was incredibly dedicated to the UFW and expected the same from all of us. Every morning at 7:30 a.m., Leroy called us to ask, "What's on your agenda for today?" We would tell him our schedule for the day, "We know we have to go out to X number of markets to do leafleting about the lettuce and grape boycotts and some of the legislation in Sacramento, and we have to go to this meeting to talk to these people." Leroy would say, "Add to that . . ." and he would add to the list. "Make sure you go to Ralph's at this time for this reason, make sure you're at Safeway at this time . . ." and so on.

Every morning, we went over the list of tasks for the day, and every night around ten or eleven, LeRoy called us to go over the checklist. "How many leaflets did you put out? How many shopping centers did you go to? Which ones were they? How many people did you call? How much money did you raise? How many volunteers did you get?" It was pretty intense work.

Volunteers who have worked with me know that I do the same thing. After every event, we have an evaluation: What did we do well? What could we do better next time? I learned that during the "No on 22" campaign. That part was good.

But we were there with a ten-month-old baby. Childcare was the main source of friction between us and the UFW. We wanted to be part of the movement and be able to spend time with our children, not just leave them somewhere while we worked all the time. We had a different idea: that the baby was a part of our lives, so she should be with us, not a stranger. Plus, babysitters were expensive. Colleen came with us to every campaign meeting.

I remember doing a speaking engagement with Colleen, who was still a baby. I could tell when people were going to start clapping or yelling at some excitement and I would put my hands over her ears so she wouldn't wake up crying.

The first year was hard, and this lifestyle put us in a lot of difficult situations as parents. For instance, I realized that whenever Colleen was nursing, she seemed to really resent it if I talked to other people. She would stop nursing completely. That meant that when people would come to our house for meetings, nursing was off the table. I don't think during that whole year we ever hired a babysitter. We took her everywhere with us. If I thought I was going to be gone for a couple of hours, I put milk aside to make sure she would be breast-fed at all times. I tried my darnedest to be a good mother to Colleen. Sometimes I set up the playpen with toys and things, but she was never satisfied. She never stayed in the playpen. She didn't sleep. She hated to sleep. She loved being with me, which was a truly lovely thing, and I tried to be a part of that in spite of everything going on. I think for a baby, it was probably a hard time because there was so much anxiety in our lives, but we were trying desperately trying to be caring, on-the-job parents for her.

When the "No on 22" campaign ended successfully, we went back to La Paz. By this time, our trailer had arrived. It was like a narrow little railcar with just the basics, but it was such an improvement from how we had been living before. We felt like we had just moved into the Beverly Hilton Hotel.

Our next assignment was to take over *El Taller Grafico*, which was the sale of posters, bumper stickers, T-shirts, and that kind of thing. Then Blase was shifted over to run the newspaper *El Malcriado*. *El Malcriado* means "the brat" in Spanish; not acting the way you are supposed to act. That was the Farm Workers. When Blase took on that project, I took over the operation of *El Taller Grafico* myself.

As soon as I found out that *El Taller Grafico* was my job, I went to the storeroom where all the posters, T-shirts, bumper stickers, and other materials were kept. It was like an earthquake had hit the room. There were boxes and papers all over the place. So my first job was to clean up and organize things. I found mail with requests for bumper stickers from three years ago with checks in the envelopes. It was a total disaster. I pulled everything out, I got it all organized, and I came up with a form letter and sent it out to all these people who had sent checks. I spent much of the year just putting things in order. No one ever seemed able to keep the books. We just kept buying things and selling them.

While I was doing that, Blase was getting *El Malcriado* out.

Blase Martin was born in June 1972. We had to go into Bakersfield to see the doctor and for the birth. On office visits, I had to wait for hours to see the doctor. I realized that the doctor was scheduling multiple patients for the same time slots, so we all had to wait and wait to be called in. I tried to talk to them about it, but they just told me to mind my business. So we all just had to sit there, waiting.

At another appointment, they did a test to tell me the precise moment when Blase Martin would be born. They didn't want me to go into labor and not make it to the hospital on time. When we went in for the test, Blase and I were still doing Lamaze, natural birth together as husband and wife. They laid me on the table and painted my stomach red with Mercurochrome, and came out with a needle that looked about twelve inches long. I saw the needle coming down, then heard the doctor say to the nurse, "I think you better take him out and give him some smelling salts." Blase was passing out and they had to take him out while they stuck the needle in me. The test determined that Blase Martin would be born on June 29.

However, Blase Martin was born on June 26, 1972. We drove to Bakersfield when I began to have labor pains and got delayed by an endless freight train. By the time we got there, there were no more beds in the maternity ward. It was a full moon, so the hospital was full. I ended up in some random room. My doctor was not on duty, so a strange doctor came in and realized I was with the United Farm Workers. He said, completely out of the blue, "Would you like to have your tubes tied while you're here?"

I was shocked. "If I did, I would have decided before now. This is not the time." I was so offended that he would ask me that. I was sure it was related to the fact that I was with the Farm Workers and his perception of us as peasant-like people.

Blase Martin was beautiful and healthy after all, so we took him up to La Paz where he met his sister, Colleen, for the first time. Birth was always a big event for the community of La Paz. We had a celebration and Cesar came to sing *"Las Mañanitas"* in honor of our new son.

By the time Blase Martin was born, I had already started a childcare co-op. Many of us women at La Paz wanted to be more involved in the work the Farm Workers were doing, but a lot of us had kids to care for. My friends had been part of a nursery co-op in Los Angeles, so I started a co-op for the women at La Paz. Each parent was assigned one day a week when they would mind all the kids so the rest of us could work. That way, each of us could work for the Farm Workers the other four days. We found a room we could use to gather all the children together and started collecting toys.

We got a tremendous amount of resistance. Much of the leadership said that this was a bourgeois endeavor and that this wasn't the way for farmworker women. We were just supposed to pitch in and bring our kids with us when we were doing things.

The women kept fighting for the co-op, arguing, "No, we really want to participate, but when we're at the office, we want to be able to devote ourselves to work, and when we're with our kids, we want them to be getting our attention."

Eventually, the leadership let us have the co-op. We drew up rules for the parents. Each parent would put in one morning per week for every child they had, and the other mornings that parent could go off and work at their other responsibilities.

Dolores Huerta lived at La Paz off and on, and she often brought her children, one or more, and just said, "I'm going off to Sacramento," or whatever, without respecting the rules of the co-op. We all knew what incredibly wonderful work she was doing. She was definitely much more into it than all of us were, even though we wanted to be.

Because I was one of the founders of the co-op, I had to bring this up to her, which didn't go over well at all. Dolores was, and is, a hero to me and many others, but we were a bit touchy about this subject.

But the childcare co-op went on. It was very successful, even though there was always a lot of hostility toward us for it.

While this was going on, we were still being sent out on other campaigns. For one campaign, we were sent back to the Valley. They had a house for us that had been previously rented by other Farm Worker organizers. The place belonged to Christine Jorgenson, a trans woman who was one of the first people widely known for having sexual reassignment surgery. Once again, it was filthy, but we made the most of it. At the time, it was felt that to be dirty was to be revolutionary. There was almost a sense of self-righteousness to it, as though we were saying, "We are revolutionaries. We don't have time to be cleaning and making ourselves look nicer. We're doing the real work here." People almost took pride in showing that they had total disdain for their house or clothes. We never bought into that, which wasn't always taken well.

The campaign was just like the "No on 22" campaign; 7:30 a.m. phone calls, leafleting, and speaking. But this time we were taking Blase Martin and Colleen. I was nursing Blase Martin so, like with Colleen, I had to nurse him, go out for three hours, come back, feed him and change him, then go back out. Fortunately, this time we did have a neighbor lady we could leave him with.

We had no furniture at all. A guy from a local church found out about us. He knew about the Farm Workers, and he asked, "Where's your furniture?"

We were so naïve. We were so determined to live by the idea that "If the farmworkers are living this way, we're going to live this way."

So he said, "Well, you need—"

I said, "We need cribs, we need everything."

He was running a kind of a thrift store called Mend for His Church, which still is in existence. He said, "Don't worry."

The next thing I knew, two cribs arrived. He sent furniture. He sent clothes. He sent all sorts of things. All of a sudden, we had a house.

We lived with another couple who also had a little girl. It was rough. Between the work and our two little babies, there was no letup at all, and certainly no sense that a mother could stay home with the children. I didn't really want to stay home, but I didn't know how I was meant to balance these two intense parts of my life. I would have liked a little more consideration from the UFW, but I didn't really know how to fight for it.

During the campaign, we were out of the house for most of the day, and only got home at night. People came to our house, dropping in, having a cup of coffee, and leaving their dirty dishes. It was a Farm Workers' house, a headquarters. I was getting angrier and angrier. I actually threw out one guy who just wanted to talk with us all the time. One night when he was over, I was working on a mailing and I knew LeRoy would call soon to go over the checklist. I said, "I have to get this mailing done. Will you help me?"

He said, "Oh no, I'm just a strategist for the far left."

Blase and I have laughed over this for so many years. He had no intention of ever doing anything at all. I was so tired and so fed up, I told him, "I don't have time for any strategy. I have my strategy. He's called LeRoy. So I'll have to ask you to leave now. I have to get on with my work." He couldn't believe it. He was so horrified. In fact, Blase was horrified; he always had a hard time saying no to anybody. But I couldn't put up with it anymore. I was under too much pressure with the kids and everything else. Honestly, we were both struggling at that point. Blase was totally at everybody's command and I needed help with the kids. We were having a hard time fitting our marriage, our kids, and our activism into our lives, and everything was piling up.

There was no time for a life. There was absolutely not a minute of time or energy left to do anything pleasurable. My friends called; we couldn't go out to dinner. I found it really oppressive, and I started realizing more clearly just how much a movement can drain everything out of a person in the name of the revolution or the cause. It was kind of like the convent lesson all over again. This was not going to stop until I stopped it. It took me a while again to start realizing that this was not going to work out so well.

But we were still going out on these campaigns. That was the good part. It was exciting, and it was definitely a noble cause. We were learning a lot. We loved doing the speaking engagements and talking about the Farm Workers, and we were really successful at it. That all felt great, and definitely kept us there for a while.

At some point, both of our kids got terrible diaper rashes. Because we had no washer or dryer, I had to go to the laundromat. We had no medical help, and the rash wasn't going away no matter what I did. Someone we knew had a doctor friend who would see us. He confirmed how severe the diaper rash was. I knew that it wasn't something we were doing. Something was going on at the laundromat—I don't know what. I knew that we had to get a diaper service so I knew I was doing everything I could for my children. I don't know how we found the money. We were still being paid for room and board and getting five dollars a week from the United Farm Workers, and we still had some money from Santa Paula. The one good thing about Santa Paula was that the salary had been good. I got the diaper service, went to the doctor, took care of the diaper rash, won the campaign, went back to La Paz, and had a big celebration.

One of my disappointments with La Paz was that I didn't really find a community there. After all the hate we endured in Santa Paula, I thought it would be glorious to be with the Farm Workers and people who thought like us. I found very little of that. It was a work-work-work mentality. We worked six days a week, at least half a day on Saturday, and at night there was more work, meetings, or something else we had to do. People had very little time. Even if they had a bit of time, there was a feeling that they should keep working. Cesar never stopped working. His top people never stopped working. So everybody followed their lead.

LeRoy, Marshall, and Jessica ran the meetings and developed

most of the strategy, though Cesar and Dolores were always there. They were open meetings; democratic. We all talked about what was going to happen, but they always had a well thought-out agenda. They did listen to us, but they were so brilliant and such good organizers that we usually did what they said.

At one meeting, we learned that the FBI had found out about threats to Cesar's life. They said there was an offer of $30,000 to kill Cesar, plus another $10,000 to destroy all the records in La Paz. The FBI representatives told us that we all had to be more security-conscious and that there had to be more vetting of people who came into the compound. When they got to the $10,000 offer for the files, everybody laughed, even Cesar. We couldn't imagine anyone paying money for those files. They were all over the floor. They were in boxes. They were of no use to anybody unless you were going to do spend a year painstakingly organizing them like I was. The files were always a mess. You could never find anything.

Helen Chavez was a very strong woman. She and Cesar had eight children that she cared for. Cesar was always gone. When everybody started laughing, she said, "You wouldn't be laughing if it was your life, would you?"

We all agreed that this was not to be taken lightly. Guards (chosen from our group) were scheduled from midnight to six o'clock in the morning. They were supposed to drive all over the Tehachapi area and our compound at La Paz to make sure nobody was breaking in to kill Cesar and destroy our files. Blase was asked to do this on Saturday nights or all day on Sundays. I put my foot down. Sunday was the only day we could have some family time, all of us together. He told them he couldn't do it. They were never the same to us after that. It felt like they decided then that they couldn't count on us anymore. We had other priorities.

At Christmastime 1972, I went in for a meeting with Dolores and Cesar. I asked if we could an extra two days off, one before Christmas Eve and one after Christmas Day, so we could go down to LA to visit Blase's parents who were in their eighties and were not well. Two days.

Dolores said, "Bourgeois. This is so bourgeois, Theresa. We don't do that. The rest of us are going to be here. And, while I'm bringing that up, when you were out on the campaign with your two babies, you got diaper service. That is not something that Farm Worker women do."

I said, "We had no washers in our place. We tried to do all the diapers at the laundromat, but the kids were getting diaper rash, and we didn't have time to do it all. We decided it was the most expedient way so we could be out there campaigning."

She said, "It's still exorbitant, and it's not what we do. It's typical Anglo bourgeois." I couldn't believe she was bringing this up.

I got my Irish up. "Dolores, I have minded your babies many times while you've been out doing things. I was happy to do it. But you brought Pampers all the time, which are much worse than a diaper service. Not only are they more expensive, but they're also not biodegradable."

Cesar was still sitting there. He interrupted, "What are Pampers?"

I realized that it did seem kind of trivial. But he had Helen to mind his children. After that incident, we got to know Dolores well, and to this day, Anyway, they said we could stay an extra day, but it was clear that our credibility went down a lot at that point.

We took the children to Blase's family's house for our big Christmas vacation. Blase's father was not happy about our living situation. He said, "What are you two doing living like that? Just because you want to help the poor doesn't mean that you need to live in these conditions. I don't want my children and grandchildren living in a trailer with an old car and no clothes to wear. It's no place to raise children, and no way to live. You can still help the poor without making yourselves and your children live like that."

I had just left La Paz, where they had told me, "You're too bourgeois, you're too rich," and here we were hearing, "You're hippies. You're still hippies." My God, Merry Christmas, everybody!

After Blase said he wouldn't go on night duty, it just kind of went downhill from there. Cesar was not as interested as he had been in *El Malcriado*. He still wanted to get the paper out, but he put Blase in charge of the Farm Workers' fleet, which consisted of junk cars that never ran, didn't have tires, didn't have this part or that part. This was an impossible job, the least desirable job in La Paz. It was not Blase's forte. It was a mean assignment.

Shortly after Cesar put Blase in charge of the fleet, we went to see Cesar and the other leaders. We said we would still like to work for the Farm Workers, but we would like to go back to work in the Valley where we could do speaking engagements; fundraising; line up supporters, sustainers, and members; and recruit farm workers. Cesar was thrilled when anybody was willing to do fundraising.

They sent us back to the Valley in the spring of 1973 to live in Mission Hills. We were excited to be out of the compound and on our own. We started a sustainer program. Volunteers were pouring in from Cal State Northridge, and we were getting a lot of calls and a lot of help.

Blase Martin was still new when we moved to Mission Hills. Colleen was almost two years old. I was still trying to be as present as possible with them, and everyone had told me that children always get a little jealous when a new baby enters the mix. I took my green stamp coupons that everyone was collecting for me, and bought Colleen a little rocking chair and a little crib with a doll. I also managed to get her a kitten so she had her own babies to take care of.

The little doll and crib worked out wonderfully, and she really enjoyed feeding her babies. The only problem was the kitten, who scratched Colleen to pieces because she wanted to "hold the baby" the way I held Blase Martin; unfortunately, we had to get rid of the cat.

We settled in and immediately got to work getting out and organizing. Once people found out Blase was in town, we started getting requests for Blase to speak on different topics from people like KPFK Radio. This was strange to me, but LeRoy stepped in and told us we weren't allowed to do that anymore. He said, "There will be one spokesperson for the Farm Workers in LA, and that's me or someone I choose. Stop accepting the speaking engagements and radio programs." It seemed like it was getting a little competitive.

We were still going, running things out of our house, when we got a letter from the office. The Farm Workers in Coachella were on a huge strike. The workers were facing terrible hardship. Cesar didn't have any money to pay the volunteers—which was what we were— so they were cutting back on all of their personnel. All the funding was cut off. They could no longer pay the room and board, medical benefits, and the five dollars a week we had been receiving. There we were with two kids and no more checks coming, and we certainly did not have a big savings account.

We didn't know what we were going to do. We went on food stamps. We tried to go on unemployment, but our salary had been so strange that they couldn't calculate our benefits, so we didn't get anything. I was really unhappy with the way this had all been handled, the abruptness of it all. It wasn't that the Coachella workers didn't need the help, they definitely did. It was the way it was done. It was not necessary and not humane. They should have said, we'll pay you for three months or six months; we'll pay you until you can get something else. But everything was just cut off with no warning.

We were really concerned about the health benefits we had lost. Then, something like a miracle happened. It seems wrong to call anything related to the Sylmar Earthquake in 1971 a miracle, but this was for us. After the earthquake, something like the Marshall Plan went into effect in that whole area to help the people. One day, the front doorbell rang. Two men were at the door. They said, "We're doing a survey for the Sylmar Earthquake. May we ask you some questions?" I found that they were trying to sign people up for a new medical plan that was being set up to help people in the area. They asked us questions to see if we qualified, and we told them we get room and board, five dollars a week, and our assets were absolutely nothing. We qualified. They said, "According to what your assets are, you wouldn't have to pay for anything."

I started taking the kids to the doctor immediately while we had the chance. We got glasses. We got orthopedic shoes for Colleen. I was getting all the benefits I could before they took them away.

I started to realize that our kids were around adults all the time. This wasn't fun for them. I drew up a flier for kids in the neighborhood, inviting them to come and play. Someone at an apartment nearby said, "Don't you know that building is all singles? There are no kids over there." Finally, I found out about the Sepulveda Parent Nursery Co-op, but it was still too early for Colleen to get into a co-op. We had moved in January and she couldn't join until September. I did call them up anyway to see if they had any kids who wanted to come over and play with us. I remember a little African American girl who came over, and there were also some kids down the street that I invited. We had a swing set that someone gave to us in the backyard. I tried to make sure Colleen and Blase Martin had something to do.

As soon as Colleen was two years and nine months old, we were able to join the Sepulveda Parent Nursery Cooperative, which meant that one parent, me or Blase, had to work one day a week at the co-op. Blase and I were also in a food co-op, and I was teaching four days a week at Santa Monica College and four nights a week at Venice Adult School. Friday was the only day we could do our co-op work, and every Friday morning, Blase and I debated about which one of us was going to go to the child co-op. Neither of us were really used to being around a lot of kids and being playful, but we learned, and it ended up teaching us a lot about parenting. I used to bring a whole bunch of kids home with me on Friday afternoons, which helped a bunch of other mothers who babysat my kids the rest of the week. On Friday afternoons, I had a whole yard full of kids. I think in a lot of ways, our kids really did have a very rich life at that time, and I must say we tried to be attentive parents in spite of how busy we were.

I set up Colleen and Blase Martin's room with a tape recorder with songs and games and stories. Colleen absolutely loved learning. I remember sitting with her, teaching her all the shapes and numbers and reading stories. She always played this little game where she had to name each shape and place them in their corresponding boxes. Of course, she understood every game she looked at in no time, so I was always searching for new things to keep her interested. Colleen quickly learned to play the tape recorder. I got her some tapes with Halloween songs and little stories for her to listen to, and soon she started making up little stories of her own as well.

Colleen started talking very early. Blase used to carry her around on his back, and one day, when she was acting as if he were her horse, she remarked matter-of-factly, "I'm beginning to like you," which was a hilarious and interesting comment.

We were still doing the work for the UFW. We had speaking engagements and other duties, we just weren't getting anything from the Farm Workers. One of our best volunteers, Tori Hill, who now works at the Library of Congress, was a student at Cal State Northridge. She helped us all the time, babysat for us, and brought her guitar to our speaking engagements. One day, she asked if it would help if she moved in. That way, she could at least pay some rent. She took the room we had been using for *El Malcriado,* which we were still putting out. Then John Gibson, a carpenter, came over and redid our garage, turning it into an office. We were adapting to the changes and still trying to make things work.

We were still on food stamps and on the welfare-type medical plan. Blase, who was handling the administration while I was handling phoning and filing, was doing whatever he could to make money. Because we didn't have any Xeroxes or adding machines, whenever Blase made a deposit at the bank, he'd say, "I need to make a copy because we send everything up to La Paz." He used the Xerox machine and adding machine at the bank. It was like his private office. The people at the bank thought this was hysterical. They would say, "Here comes Mr. Businessman again." We ran the whole program and actually had a fun time, singing union songs with Tori, people coming and going all the time. But we knew this couldn't last forever.

CHAPTER 6

Transitions: A Run for the Assembly, Movies, and Central America

We knew we had to start making some money. I got a job first, at Kennedy Adult School in the Valley. Then Blase's friend at Cal State Northridge, Larry Littwin, said, "We need you to teach over here." So Blase went back into teaching part-time at Cal State. That was our first little break away from the Farm Workers.

We moved from our apartment in Mission Hills to a house in Reseda in January of 1974. Blase's mother gave us $3,000 to put toward the down payment on the house. We also had $3,000 we had saved from our teaching jobs, so we were able to make a down payment of $6,000. After we moved, we just sort of drifted away from the Farm Workers.

Then Blase decided to run for the state assembly. I was really angry. Blase kept saying so and so is going to be the fundraiser and so and so is going to be the campaign manager, but I knew that I was going to wind up being the campaign manager. He kept taking on more responsibilities when my plate was already full. We had these two little kids to worry about, I was trying to get back into teaching, and we were still in the throes of setting up our new house. We had no furniture of our own, Blase Martin was just about one and a half years old, and Colleen was around three. So yes, I was mad. He ran for office four times, and every time he ran we ended up owing $5,000 in campaign expenses.

We went back up to see Cesar again about Blase's campaign, and he said, "That's a good idea. We need people in the legislature. You get your campaign started and you can count on us." They now had all the printing presses that Blase had bought for *El Malcriado*. Cesar said, "We'll run all your bumper stickers and we'll do your posters and all of your literature and everything like that. That's the big expense of a campaign, so you won't have to worry about that. We'll help."

Theresa and Blase with their two children, 1974.

We got back and Blase started his campaign. I didn't choose to be a campaign manager—it wasn't the plan—but since we couldn't hire one, it ultimately fell to me, as I had predicted.

We started scouting around for an office, starting out at our home as usual. We ran into a man named Glen Buchannan at a Democratic club meeting. He gave us a free office space. We started working, getting the maps and books, and learning how to campaign all over again.

We went to all the Democratic clubs and Unitarian churches to speak and gather support. When we called Cesar to check in on our posters and literature, he didn't answer. He never returned our calls. He never even told us that he had changed his mind, which was a great disappointment. I was terribly angry at the way he did it. I knew he was busy, and I would have understood if he had said something like, "I know what I said, but we're in the middle of the Coachella strike and we've got all these other things going on," but there was no explanation. I wrote Cesar a letter, essentially explaining that it would have been fine if he had changed his mind, but at least he could have had the courtesy to let us know. We, and the campaign, were left to fend for ourselves.

We had raised some money and had some signs made, and we recruited at least a hundred volunteers in no time. People made professional signs for us. We started organizing the human billboard campaign, sending people to freeway off-ramps with signs that read: *Blase Bonpane for State Assembly*. It was amazing how much support we got from the community. We always had enough volunteers.

Even though I was against it at first, once we got the campaign going, it was exciting. People flocked to the headquarters to donate money and supplies. One woman, Mildred Simon, came in and found out that we didn't have paper clips, paper, or folders. Mildred told us, "Go to my stationery store and get that stuff." Patty McManus, a young woman in her early twenties, took care of the kids full-time.

One day, we came home and Colleen was sitting in a chair with her arms folded. She said, "I don't like it. I don't like it." I asked her what she didn't like and she said, "I don't like that you and Daddy are gone all the time and I'm alone."

I said, "You're with Patty."

She said, "No, I'm alone because you're not here."

She was really adamant about it. I sat and talked with her, trying to explain why we were gone so much. Daddy had run for this office and we had to go to these speaking engagements.

She kept saying, "I don't like it," and started to cry. "I miss you when you're gone all the time."

It broke my heart. I tried to talk to her about it and promised we'd try not to be gone as much. So she said something to the effect of, "I understand." It was a really hard time for the kids and for us.

We had to be gone so much, and of course, when we were home, we were on the phone all the time. Fortunately, the kids loved Patty and had a great time with her, so that made things a bit easier.

Theresa as a young mother of two, 1975.

At the time, Jerry Brown was running for Secretary of State. He asked for an endorsement for his campaign. I can't remember now what it was that Jerry had done that we didn't approve of, but when his office called and asked for our endorsement, we said no. We also didn't ask him to endorse Blase. We had a rather purist attitude about things. We kept running into him at all the Democratic clubs, but he didn't forgive us for a long time.

Jerry's father, Pat Brown, the former governor, knew Blase's father. One night, we were all at a big Italian American event with all the diplomats and politicians. All the candidates were allowed to say a few words. Blase's father ran into Pat Brown and introduced us.

Brown said, "I know Blase. He came and visited me once."

When Blase was still a priest, he had visited Pat Brown to see if he would appoint his father to a judgeship, which he later did.

Pat Brown pulled Blase and me aside to chat, saying, "I know a lot about you and what you've done. I think it's great." At some point in the conversation, he confided, "I just wish my son would find someone to marry. I think he'd be a lot happier if he did." It was nice, and a bit funny, that he shared with us this little confidence about his son, Jerry.

During this period, I dressed like a waif most of the time. We were on a Farm Workers budget, and clothes were not a priority. In fact, we were probably the neatest of the group because we were trying to appeal to the establishment, but still we had no clothes to speak of. We now had these fancy events to attend, and we needed appropriate clothes. We could always find something for Blase, but it was much harder for me as a woman. There's so much more pressure placed on women to look and dress right. I always borrowed clothes. When I got home on the evening of this big fancy Italian American night, I realized I had nothing to wear. I had been campaigning all day, running the human billboard campaign, throwing signs in the car, and lugging signs and literature around. I asked one of the volunteers if I could borrow her dress for that night. She brought me a long dress that, thankfully, fit me. It turned out that everybody was wearing long dresses that night, so it was appropriate. But I didn't have a jacket or sweater.

Blase's mother called that afternoon to see if we were all set. Because we were going with Blase's parents, they were concerned with how we would look to all their friends. We said that we were fine. Blase's mother asked, "What's Theresa going to wear?" because she was always concerned about whether I looked appropriate for the occasion, which I seldom did. Blase told her that I had a dress, but needed a sweater. She said, "Come over. I've got a lot of sweaters and jackets. Tell her not to give it another thought and come over." I thought she had some sort of other agenda on her mind. We dashed out of the house. Because we had been campaigning, I hadn't had time to get the car washed, so it was a mess.

Just after we arrived at Blase's parents' house, Blase's sister Fleurette, who was always gorgeous and always dressed elegantly, got out of her shining BMW wearing her fur coat. Then Aunt Gale and Uncle Jack arrived in their shining Jaguar. She was also in a fur coat. We were late, so everyone was in a hurry. Blase's mother said, "Come over here," and opened the trunk and handed me a fur jacket. She said, "Try this on. I think it will fit." Everyone was waiting and watching this performance.

I said, "I can't wear this fur coat." This was before we really got into the fur campaign, but it just didn't feel right. It wasn't me. I said, "Thank you, but you know, I can't wear this."

They all said, "Oh, it's beautiful. It's lovely. It's so you. You have to wear it."

I repeated, "It really isn't me."

Blase's mother said, "Well, try this one on." It was yet another fur jacket.

Everyone had me trying on all these different fur jackets. I kept saying, "No, it's not me. I'm just not comfortable."

Blase's mother said, "Well, you're Mrs. Bonpane now, so you'll have to like it."

I put my foot down. "But I'm *Theresa* Bonpane, and it's just not me."

The men didn't say much. I know that Blase's father didn't care about the way I dressed, but he didn't say anything. Blase's mother was really very good-natured about it. She conceded, "All right, all right. I understand. Just do me one favor then. You don't have to wear a fur coat, but will you please carry this bag instead of that cloth shoulder bag?" I agreed to that.

Blase was running against Tom Bane and Jack McGrath. Mc-

Grath was a John F. Kennedy type. He was smart, handsome, sharp, and knew everything about politics. Everyone was quite sure that he was going to win. Occasionally, I'd have to speak on Blase's behalf, because he'd have to give a talk somewhere else and couldn't be at two places at once. McGrath always came over and said, "Boy, Blase is so lucky. If you weren't running his campaign, I'd love to have you run mine," and all this other Irish flattery. He would say, "You two are wonderful. If I wasn't running, you'd be the ones I'd want to win," and all of this other blarney.

But, no. McGrath didn't win, and neither did Blase. Tom Bane won the campaign. We thought he was corrupt. He was very involved with Alan Robbins, a corrupt state senator who was later convicted on racketeering and tax evasion. They were in real estate together.

Blase was undaunted. His need to be doing something worthwhile with every minute of his life was so generous, so sincere. He was overwhelmingly committed to it. There was a feeling that every minute of his life was precious and that he was only here for a short amount of time, so he had to make every minute count. I think it was really important to him to know that he at least tried to change things.

The campaign drew us back into a lot of new political issues. It wasn't just the Farm Workers anymore. We were back into war issues and economic issues. The campaign had mostly dealt with domestic problems. Watergate was exploding. When we went out speaking to the public, we talked about whatever they wanted to hear.

When it was over in June, there we were again, with no money and $5,000 in campaign debt.

We settled back into our home in Reseda and got right back to work. We needed to pay our bills and make a living. Cal State Northridge hired Blase part-time here and there. He was always getting in trouble—the minute they heard he was teaching for a semester, the students would flock to his classes. The administration said that he was so popular because was teaching socialism, so they got rid of him, but the students kept writing appeals to get him back again. So he was occasionally working, but most of the time he wasn't.

I had gone back into the LA city schools in Adult Education and met Ralph Self, the principal at Kennedy High School in Granada Hills. Ralph had a really good impression of ex-nuns, and the minute I started telling him my history, he said, "Absolutely, we're going to get you a job."

I told him about my husband and his campaign, and he said, "If he's anything like you, we'll get him a job as well." By September 1974, we both had jobs in the Adult Education School, teaching mostly English as a Second Language (ESL). I taught some Spanish as well. I can't remember if Blase was teaching at Northridge as well, but we were both trying to get as many jobs and hours as possible. We started paying our bills.

I went full-swing back into teaching because I knew that I would likely become the main breadwinner for the family, which meant that I would also need to get health benefits for all of us. Blase was still doing a few different things then, but nothing really steady. I was made the chair of the department. I joined the union, United Teachers of Los Angeles (UTLA), and became the union representative at the school. Once my boss found out I was the UTLA representative, he became a little colder to me, little by little, distancing himself from me. I think he thought I had betrayed him because he really did bend over backward to help me, having me take tests so I could become vice principal or principal of the school and inviting me to a lot of the upper-level meetings.

Blase and I both took the exam to become a school administrator, thinking, "What harm could it do?" I could barely work through the paperwork of preparing for the exam. The forms were horrendous. Blase did the forms for us and we both took the test. I passed the test, but Blase didn't, which was kind of a shocker.

The administration at Cal State Northridge did horrible things to Blase during that time. The students wouldn't let the administration alone because they kept cutting Blase's classes, so they eventually hired Blase. They gave him one class at 8:00 a.m. and one class at 8:00 p.m., which made it nearly impossible for him to do anything else. We later found out that the professors at Cal State were really upset that Blase's classes were so popular—standing room only. Meanwhile, the other professors could barely get enough students to keep a class going. Blase taught his first class at Cal State in the morning, then he taught at Mission Hills College in the middle of the day, then he headed back to Cal State to teach his evening class. He was constantly traveling to get to his three jobs.

Blase had bronchitis all the time that year. We only had one car, so most days he biked between Northridge and Mission Hills College, which is just about the entire length of the Valley. His doctor told him, "You cannot bike that far in the San Fernando Valley." He said it was like smoking five packs of cigarettes a day. We thought about the smog in the Valley and what it was doing to Blase and the kids, so we decided to move to the Westside. In 1977, we moved to Mar Vista. I was still teaching at Kennedy, commuting to the Valley, and Blase was still teaching at Northridge. We sold the Reseda house, which had doubled in value since we bought it. We got it for $29,000 and sold it for $60,000. We found a house in Mar Vista for $60,000 and moved there.

In 1974, Blase's mother died. Blase's father was distraught. He felt totally abandoned. After a couple of years, he met a beautiful woman who was sixty-five. He was around eighty. It wasn't clear in the beginning that she was after his money, but later on, it became obvious. This was really hard on Blase and his siblings. She started trying to turn Blase's father against his kids, telling him, "They're not doing anything for you." He became increasingly paranoid against us. The woman also had him on all sorts of medicine, like Percodan, that would make him more paranoid. She tried to confuse him, control him, and own him. She got a valet in the house and told him that we were the "bad, horrible family," and that he shouldn't let any of us in without checking with her. She took over his life entirely. By this time, she was using his credit cards. Six weeks before he died, she took him to Las Vegas when he was very ill, married him, and changed the will. He died in July of 1977.

At the same time, my mother was very ill. She was eighty-four and sick all the time. I was traveling back and forth between New York and LA until she died in May of 1977. After she died, my father was so lonely that I went back to Troy to pick him up so he wouldn't be snowbound during the winter. I took him with me on the first plane ride of his entire life. He was eighty-nine years old. He lived with us from November until March. The following November, I brought him back out to Los Angeles where he died in December 1978.

During these years, we were focused on taking care of our parents and working to get our debts paids, but we were still trying to find time for political work. I did a lot with the Coalition for Economic Survival, a group that was helping poor people get food and find adequate rentals. The goal was basically economic survival for people who were struggling.

Blase and I had both been very interested in Latin America in the years before we went to work for the Farm Workers, especially since we had both spent so much time there. Blase was active in a group called Committee on Latin American Solidarity (COLAS) when I met him. He had also been involved in a group called Avoid Vietnam in Latin America (AVILA) which had merged into COLAS. I recall those groups as more theoretical and academic than activist, though there were always people who wanted to change things. I don't remember a lot of demonstrations or anything like that. I remember going to meetings, talking about what was wrong, writing letters, and that kind of stuff. While we were in Santa Paula and in La Paz with the Farm Workers, we were not active with any of these groups at all. They must have disintegrated shortly after we left. At least, I don't remember hearing about them anymore.

In 1973 Salvador Allende was assassinated in Chile. We were in Mission Hills and just winding down with the Farm Workers. I was still thinking of going for my master's and had just started taking a class at Cal State Northridge at the time. I remember that morning that I went to Cal State for my class. I guess I hadn't read the newspaper yet, and when I got there, Larry Littwin, the professor, was almost crying in class. He said, "Did you all hear about the news this morning? Allende was assassinated." We were devastated by it, because there had been so much hope for Chile itself, but also hope that Chile would be a model for other countries.

I don't really remember the specific time we started getting involved with Central America. We were getting an increasing number of calls from people in Nicaragua about what was going on with Somoza. The rebels had organized the Sandinista National Liberation Front (FSLN) and the Sandinista Revolution was in full swing. El Salvador was also starting to flare up. We started organizing and trying to get the word out, which meant speaking engagements, sending out letters, and things like that. No one seemed to know or care about what was going on. It took a long time for us to really get the word out about what was happening. Blase was doing a lot of speaking engagements by 1975, and by 1976, Blase was working with the Nicaraguan Solidarity Group at Cal State Northridge. In 1978 a group called the Committee in Solidarity with the People of El Salvador (CISPES) was organized back East. A woman named Ruth Tartar came to Blase about starting a local branch. I helped organize the office. We did fundraising for CISPES, and we were also working with Medical Aid for El Salvador, for whom we also did some fundraising, as well as the Central American Resource Center (CARECEN) and *El Rescate*.

By 1977 everybody was coming to our house for meetings. Martin Sheen had just done *Apocalypse Now*, and a cinematographer asked us if he could show Martin a film on the death squads in El Salvador at our house. It was one of the first films to come out that showed the massacres that were going on in El Salvador. That was the first time we met Martin. He was just delightful. He was so fun to be with, and he could not have been more generous. He really wanted to help out. Martin has remained a good friend. He was immediately interested in what we were trying to do, and he said, "Count on me. I'll do everything I can to get this video out."

We were all committed to finding different ways to talk about Latin America to a North American audience. Film was one of the ways. Around the same time, we met Glen Silber, who had done a documentary about the anti-Vietnam War movement called *The War at Home* and was working on another documentary called *El Salvador: Another Vietnam*. He asked if we could distribute his movie as well, and suddenly we were the big "Hollywood distributor people." We knew Martin Sheen, so people thought we knew everybody. I started doing fundraising for *El Salvador: Another Vietnam*, which was my first real fundraiser for El Salvador. Everybody was coming to us with their own projects. Along the way, we met Robert M. Young and Edward James Olmos. All of these people were interested in films on some aspect of the work we were doing.

At the same time, we were involved with several different people who wanted to make movies about us. It had begun in 1970 when a guy named Léo Malek came to our house to talk to Blase. He was a filmmaker of sorts; at that time more in name than by output. He wanted to make a movie about Blase's life. He said he was going to fundraise for the project. He started interviewing Blase, and that started the whole process. Léo and Blase came up with a script; Herb Magidson gave ten thousand dollars to the project and they started bringing it around to studios to see if they could get it produced. It didn't get very far, and they shelved the project.

Bill Norton, a very popular filmmaker, brought the idea back to life in 1977. He wanted to do a film about Blase's experiences in the Guatemalan revolution. He just wanted to devour Blase. He had heard about the script Blase and Léo Malek had done and he wanted to push it further. He put some money into the project and started rewriting the script. Bill ran into some other problems and the project died again. By this time I was so bored with the whole movie thing. I thought, "Forget it. We've got too many other things to do."

Theresa and Blase at Sundance, 1982.

Then a film producer named Moctesuma Esparza heard about it and said, "I want to see if I can get this accepted at Sundance." The Sundance Institute had just started in '81. He said, "They're looking for good scripts, and I'm going to see if I can get this accepted as one of their projects."

So he did. We sent in all the material and they had a couple of interviews with us before they accepted us as one of their projects. They invited us to come to Sundance for a month in '82. We went up there with the kids. That's when I did the first transcription of this whole story. Bob (Robert M.) Young was our screenwriter. Sundance Institute's goal was to teach and support people working in film, so they would give film professionals whatever they needed. If you wanted to be an actor or an actress, then Robert Redford himself would help show you how to act out whatever part you were working on. In fact, he offered to play the part of the priest in our film if we got it moving along.

Theresa and Blase at Sundance with Robert Redford, 1982.

All of these people were working on it. I'm not a writer and I'm definitely not a screenwriter, so I kept thinking, "How am I supposed to be helping out?" They minded my kids full-time, and I felt like I was supposed to be doing something. That's when I started recording this story. They could pull from that, extract whatever they wanted. I sat in a room all by myself, went back to second grade, and tried to go through the whole story.

I learned then that convent thing still wasn't out of my system. When I got to that part, I broke down sobbing. They transcribed the tape up there and the poor transcriptionist put things like, "Pause, crying." After a while, she just put "Pause."

It was a real catharsis. I left the convent in '67, and I felt so liberated the minute I walked out that I never had any guilt about it. But at least once a month I had a dream where I was still asking, "Should I leave? Shall I stay? If I leave, will God punish me?" Sometimes I dreamed that I was still in the habit and I would arrive somewhere, like a dance or something, and forget that I still had my habit on. It was like my worlds were mixing up in my dreams.

At Sundance, everything just seemed to come out, all of this stuff that I hadn't dealt with entirely.

Robert Redford and all these big names from Hollywood were there, but this was the more idealistic part of the film industry. They wanted to support different kind of films and different kinds of filmmakers. They didn't see our film as a political film, they just thought of it as a worthwhile story. We got a lot of interest while we were there. A lot of people were really excited about it.

Bob Young, who was our writer, was our industry representative. It came out that he had too many other projects going at this time. On top of that, Bob got a job offer to do a movie about the pope going on vacation called *Saving Grace*.

When we got back to town, Bob Young and another producer, Michael Hausman, became interested in the movie again. They brought the script to a ton of different people. Martin Sheen had said that if we did it, he would be happy to play the priest. We met with Jane Fonda, hoping she would play the nun. Jon Voight was going to play something. All kinds of people were interested in it.

We went to see a lot of top names in the industry and many were interested, it seemed, but there were always some things that they wanted to change. After we met with this one producer, we thought he might be the one. He had read it and said, "You've got to come back." For some reason, Martin came with us to the second meeting. We got into the producer's office and he said, "Look, I love this story. It's fantastic." Then he said, "There are just three things, though, that we'd have to change before I would go ahead with it. Number one, you have to go a little easier on the US government. There's a lot of stuff about the US government's role in what's going on; we'd have to cut some of that. And you definitely can't say all that stuff about the Guatemalan government, because they're our friends. And third, the nun and the priest really have to go to bed together. We have to show them having an affair while she's still in her habit."

Blase and I were sitting there listening to all this. Martin stood right up and said, "That's it. We're outta here. We're not going to have any part of any of that."

The producer protested, "Wait a minute. Wait a minute. Let's talk about this a little bit."

"No, not if those are the conditions," replied Martin.

The producer said, "I'll tell you what. If you don't want to be part of it with these changes, I'll buy the script from you. One hundred thousand dollars."

Martin was not moved. "Absolutely not. That story is precious and it's going to stay that way. It's going to retain its purity." So we walked out of there.

Later we kidded Martin, "Gee, thanks a lot! We just had a chance to get a hundred thousand dollars for our script and you just had to walk out?" We all had a good laugh about it.

What happened with that producer seemed to happen everywhere we went. Everyone wanted to change something, but had we made those changes, it would no longer have been our story. We never did get the movie made, as it turned out.

We didn't have time to feel bad about the movie—we were doing too much work with Central America.

CHAPTER 7

El Salvador, Nicaragua, and the Office of the Americas

The situation in Central America was rapidly growing worse. I was still teaching in the Valley and I had gotten a job at Santa Monica City College. We started getting messages from people in Latin America saying that things were really heating up there. They asked: can you help? We were still in touch with AVILA, CISPES, Medical Aid to El Salvador, CARECEN, and *El Rescate*. We weren't really the activists in the groups, but we were helping to keep things going. We were constantly having meetings at our house in Mar Vista.

Sometime around 1978 we got a phone call from a woman from El Salvador. I'm not sure if she was a nun or if she had just been living with nuns. She said she was coming to LA and had been told to get in touch with the Bonpanes. She told us she had some important information she wanted to get out about what was going on in El Salvador. We said, "Okay. Come on over." Blase went to the airport to pick her up.

When she got to our house, she was all bundled up. She said, "I'm going to tell you something, but first, look at my watch."

It was about eight hours behind the current time. We said, "Oh, your watch isn't working."

She said, "I'll tell you what happened."

When the massacres started in El Salvador, the death squads dropped decapitated bodies in the city; body parts were scattered all around. It was ghoulish. They were warning people what would happen if they protested. She had started taking pictures of these bodies and collecting other people's photos as well. None of those images were coming to the United States, so she decided she needed to come here to get these photos out to the American media.

When she left El Salvador, the security was unbelievable. Anyone caught doing something the government didn't approve of was likely to join the bodies in the streets. The woman pasted the photos to her body and covered them in layers of clothes. I forget what her disguise was; she either put on a habit or simply tried to look pregnant. When she got to the airport, security was inspecting everybody. She was trembling. At some point, she was told to step out of line. They must have caught onto her somehow. They told her to go into another room and get undressed so they could examine her. That was when her watch stopped. Her heart stopped too. When she entered the room, a woman told her to take off her clothes. She did. The security woman looked at her up and down and said, "Get your clothes back on. Get out of here. Hurry up." She just pretended she didn't see what she just saw. She was letting her go. When the woman arrived in LA, she was still in a state of shock. She was terrified.

She asked us, "Can you get me on the radio on KPFK?"

We always tried to connect people with the media. We brought her to a friend of ours at the *Los Angeles Times*. We took her around to other reporters so she could show them her pictures. That was really the beginning of our Salvadoran work.

This was when the children were starting to speak up about what we were doing. One day when I took Colleen to ballet class, she said, "What do you want me to be when I grow up?"

I said, "I just want you to be a good person. Whatever you want to be is fine, so long as you're a good person who cares about others and the poor."

She said, "Well, I've been thinking." We had been working for CISPES and doing a lot of fundraisers for them. She must have been nine or ten then. She said, "I know one thing, I'm not going to be a full-time worker for CISPES."

I think she agreed with what we were doing and understood, but she was also kind of bored with it. Our activism had been such a big part of her life, and I think she was sick of all the meetings, all the people in our house talking about this stuff all the time.

She said, "Maybe if I get rich or famous I'll give some money to CISPES, but I'm not going to work as you and Daddy do for CIS-PES." She was figuring out what she wanted to with her life. It was going to be something worthwhile, she was sure of that, as was I, but it wasn't going to be volunteering for CISPES.

Blase Martin was always more interested in being part of the revolution.

Theresa with the Peace Team against the Contra War, 1979.

The children were aware that we didn't have as many material goods as everybody thought we should have. I told them, "The reason we don't have more is that we're devoted to helping the people of El Salvador," or to helping the Farm Workers, or whatever it was that we were working on at the time. "So we don't have much money for ourselves because our money goes to the cause, to helping others."

One day when Blase Martin came home, we were getting our hardwood floors refinished. He said, "What's this?"

I said, "We're getting the floors refinished."

He said, "I thought all of our money was supposed to go to El Salvador."

In December 1980, a woman who ran a travel agency approached Blase about coleading a delegation to Cuba with a fairly famous woman named Rose Chernin. Rose was a wonderful woman who had been a brilliant organizer, but she was now eighty-six years old and her mind was not as clear as it had once had been. Blase had never led a delegation before, and organizing was not his strong suit. Nevertheless, he agreed to do it. Traveling to Cuba was not dangerous, so we decided to take the kids. Colleen was ten and Blase Martin was eight. Blase had been to Cuba a number of times, but it would be the first time that the kids and I had gone.

The woman who ran the travel agency and her daughter were also going on the trip. She had done a lot of political work organizing Cuban and Russian trips in addition to the more normal trips that people usually take. We assumed that she was really the one in charge and that she wanted Blase along as political backup.

There were thirty-five or forty people in our group. We flew to Mexico City and spent the first night there. While we were in Mexico City we saw people on the street begging and with their little babies in their arms, and Blase Martin said, "This place needs a revolution." He was always picking up our language.

When we arrived in Cuba the next day, we realized that one woman had been left behind in Mexico City. Another woman's luggage didn't arrive. We started calling airlines and waiting for airplanes to come in, hoping to meet both the missing woman and the missing bags. Eventually, both arrived. Our poor kids were already worn out from hanging around the airports all day. Blase had started the trip with a bad cold, and by this point it had turned into bronchitis bordering on pneumonia. I realized that the travel agent wasn't leading, Rose couldn't lead, and Blase was too sick to do anything. I said to myself, "Uh-oh, we'd better get our act together here."

There was no one else to step up, so I thought, "Okay, then I'm in charge." I realized we needed a system. Right away, I started taking attendance. Our host in Cuba didn't seem to have his act together either. He was showing us around, and people were already saying, "I don't want to go there, I want to go here," or, "I thought we were going to see these kinds of places," or, "I thought this was going to be a more political group." Everybody had something to say about what they didn't like about the delegation.

I called a meeting to see what was wrong and what we were going to do about it. At the meeting, Joyce Fisk, a volunteer I knew well, kept giving me the eye as if to say, "You and I better leave and go someplace to figure something out." Anyway, I took all of their complaints and suggestions and said I'd talk with our Cuban leader to see what we could do. Then Joyce met me and said, "You know, I have some suggestions. I think you and I better be in charge." Right away, I realized I had a coleader. Joyce was incredible and extremely perceptive. Basically, Joyce and I took over as leaders.

The Bonpane family, 1982.

We had arrived three days before Christmas. Blase was so sick that a doctor had to come to our hotel room. I had a little something too. The kids were a little disappointed. It was Christmas, their dad was really sick, and the Cubans didn't even acknowledge the Christmas holiday. I had brought along a few little Christmas presents for them, and I tried to do some Christmassy stuff so they wouldn't feel like they were missing too much. They were the only two little kids on the whole delegation, so they didn't have anyone else to talk to or play with. They weren't interested in the political talk or the delegations.

Joyce and I got everything organized. We worked out a better itinerary. In the end, everybody pitched in and we had a wonderful delegation. The kids eventually got into it as well when they got to go horseback riding on the beach and we started meeting other kids. It was an incredible experience. It moved me to see what the United States' intervention had done to the people of Cuba and how long-lasting it had been. New Year's Eve was the anniversary of Cuba's revolution. New Year's Day was our wedding anniversary. Blase and I had been married ten years. We had our anniversary celebration as Cuba had theirs. It was perfect. We were at a great hotel where there were internationalists from all over the world. At one point, there was a big dance where everybody held hands and danced wildly around the room.

In Cuba, everything was rationed. Our friends Pauline and Richard Saxon, who had started the group Physicians for Social Responsibility, were with us on the trip. Blase Martin and Colleen were sitting with them at breakfast. We were served little demitasse cups of coffee, and we were only allowed one cup per person. When a waiter came over to fill up the demitasse cups, Pauline said, "Blase Martin, leave your cup up and take the coffee so I can have a second cup. And Colleen, you do the same for Richard." The kids left their cups up, the waiter gave them both coffee, and they gave it to the Saxons.

The second morning this happened, Blase Martin came to me and said, "Mom, Pauline is exploiting me."

I said, "What do you mean, Blase?"

He told me what had happened, and he said, "She doesn't know that the Cubans don't have enough money for everybody to have more than one cup of coffee. She's only supposed to have one cup, and she's taking mine so she can have two."

Pauline came over to me later and told me the same story. She said, "I told him, 'Blase, it's okay because they've already ground the beans and they've already made the coffee. It's okay.'"

He wasn't having it. He said, "No, no, no."

Later in the trip, Blase Martin said to me, "Look. All these houses are unpainted. How come their houses look so bad?"

I explained to him, "It's because they put all their money into medical care for their people, schools for their kids to learn in, and these wonderful childcare facilities. They put all their money into those things, and there's none left over to paint the houses."

He thought for a moment, then said, "Well, why isn't the whole world socialist then?" He really understood these concepts very quickly.

I remember when we got back from the delegation, the kids had missed some school because their Christmas break was already over. I gave them a choice: "When you give the school your excuse, you can do one of two things. You can say you were in the Caribbean and that's why you're coming back to school late, or you can say you were in Cuba. But a lot of teachers won't like to hear that you went to Cuba. They might think that we're communists or bad people, and they might treat you differently because of it." I could handle that judgment, and in fact, I told all the principals in the schools where I was teaching that I was going to Cuba. But I didn't think the kids should have to deal with that unless they were ready for it. I don't remember what Colleen said, but Blase Martin, who was only eight, announced that he would tell everybody where he went, because then people would ask why he went to Cuba, and he'd get a chance to tell everyone why Cuba was a good country and why we needed a revolution in this country.

Blase was often called on to do things for the anti-Somoza movement for Nicaragua. In 1979, Blase and I went to a conference in Mexico where finally people were beginning to recognize that we needed to do something about what was happening in Nicaragua. When Blase went back for a second meeting, he met Rosario Murillo, who was the wife of Sandinista leader Daniel Ortega. She wanted us to help get the support of celebrities for the Sandinista cause.

When we returned home, Manuel Valle, a Nicaraguan exile from Somoza's regime and a representative of the FSLN, called Blase and told him that the Sandinistas needed a support group. We started running the Nicaraguan support office out of our home. Soon, we started getting similar phone calls about El Salvador, saying that they needed a support group, so we added that to the work we were doing from our house.

This was an extremely difficult time for my marriage. I wasn't sure that Blase and I were going to continue. He was gone all the time. He was always giving talks. There was no time for a home life, and I was becoming increasingly resentful. I was working several jobs and taking care of the kids, and I was just stretched really thin. I was teaching three-hour classes in Adult Ed four nights a week and four mornings a week.

I also felt the pressure of being the main breadwinner. Blase struggled to hold down a job, so I was not only the main financial supporter, but I was also responsible for the medical benefits we got through my jobs. I was becoming so angry that it felt like we never got our lives balanced out. Anger wears you out faster than anything else, and we were really struggling for a lot of those years.

As I've mentioned, Blase could never say no to anyone. In 1979 we went on our first vacation with the kids. We went to Yosemite. I remember how nice it was. Someone had lent us a little van and we were planning to camp out by this beautiful river, which was something we had never done. It was so restful, so peaceful. But Blase was always off making his phone calls. He said, "Manuel Valle called me.

I have to go back to LA. They think Samosa is going to be overthrown any day now. It's inevitable, and it will happen in the next week or two. PBS wants to do something on it." Manuel didn't speak very good English, so he depended entirely on Blase to do all his speaking engagements for him.

I had just had it. I said, "No, we're not going back. I don't care. If we go back, I'm out of this. I'm not going to continue this relationship." I was really that upset, but we ended up going back because he had to be on PBS. Sure enough, within a week Somoza was overthrown. July 17, 1979. Within three days, Manuel Valle was invited back to Nicaragua because they wanted him to be the consul in Los Angeles. He asked Blase to go down with him. This was the first time I didn't even help Blase pack.

I just said, "You pack for yourself. I've had it." Of course, I cared about the movement and was happy about the triumph, but I was upset about what all of this was doing to our lives.

While he was there, Rosario Murillo, Daniel Ortega's wife, asked Blase to bring a delegation of celebrities down to Nicaragua so that we could get some publicity about what the Sandinistas were doing and what the people had gone through. When he came back, of course, he immediately became the spokesperson.

I was asked to go to Nicaragua a couple of weeks later with Bill Norton and his wife Ellie, who were screenwriters. They had given the Sandinistas fifty thousand dollars. The minute the triumph established the Sandinistas in power, they wanted to go to Nicaragua to talk with the new government about what they were going to do to help in solidarity. They asked me to go as their translator. You never knew what they were going to come up with next.

As it turned out, only Ellie and I went. While we were flying down, I learned more about what they really wanted. I thought they wanted to see how they could continue to help the Sandinistas, but I learned that they wanted to see if the Sandinistas would give some of the fifty thousand dollars to the IRA. I literally found this out as we were landing. This was not something I wanted to be a part of. I didn't want to be involved in shipping arms around the world.

As we were flying into Sandino Airport, I just cried. My son Blase always used to ask me, "How come all the stuff on your bumper stickers and everything you support loses all the time?" I couldn't believe that for once in our lives we had won. We had been working for the Sandinistas for two years. To come in and see Sandino Airport was so incredibly moving and exciting. The Sandinistas had already started their literacy program. This was two weeks after the triumph. People were still going around with their guns and their camouflage outfits. The soldiers, everybody, the whole country was in an uproar, but it was positive energy.

Jessie Jackson, Ernesto Cardenal, others at an OOA meeting, 1983.

The next thing I knew, we got a phone call that officials from the new government were going to meet us at the Intercontinental Hotel where we were staying. Manuel Valle was there to meet us. He had been appointed Nicaraguan consul in Los Angeles. When he walked into the consulate, the previous consul just handed him the keys and said, "Here are the keys. You're the new consul." Then he walked out.

The person who came to visit was Tomás Borge, the minister of the interior. He had been tortured by the Somozaistas. When he took over, he went to see his torturer. The whole country was wondering what he was going to do to the guy who had tortured him. Everybody knew that Tomás was going to visit him in prison.

Tomás went in and said, "You remember me?"

"Yeah, I do."

"You remember what you did to me?"

"Yeah."

"Are you wondering what I'm going to do to you?"

"Yeah."

Tomás said, "I forgive you in the name of the new Nicaragua. You must fight for this country."

That was the subject of Jackson Browne's song, "My Personal Revenge."

Tomás, with about eight security guards, brought us to his room in the hotel. By this time, Bill had arrived and joined us. We didn't know he was coming. I knew that they were going to ask about the arms meant to go to Ireland. I had to say to them and to Tomás Borge and his bunch of guards that I wanted to clarify that I was only there as their translator. I didn't know what they were going to be asking for. I wanted them to make their request however they wanted to make it, but I didn't want anyone to think it was something I was also pushing for. Blase and I had already built up a lot of credibility with Rosario and Daniel and everybody and it was not built on something like this. I was clear that this was not what I was there for.

They asked that guns be sent to Ireland. Tomás Borge said, "Look, there's no way. If we send a cockroach over the border, they're going to get us. They have so much surveillance. We cannot win what we have just won for our country by doing anything like this. That would bring the United States down on us as fast as can be. We just cannot risk it right now. We will be looking for ways to help other solidarity movements. We'll do the best we can, but we are not going to deal in any kind of arms or anything like that."

Our friends didn't like that. They didn't agree, but they accepted it.

That was my introduction to the new Nicaragua.

Ellie and I stayed for a week or so. I couldn't get over how exciting it all was. Everything was so marvelous. One night they had a big sign up that said, "Disco Dancing Tonight at the Intercontinental." Ellie was such a purist. She said, "Humph, cultural imperialism! I would never go in and do disco dancing. And with the Sandinistas in power and disco dancing—" She was horrified. When we went into the lobby, we saw all the Sandinistas entering the dance hall, so I said, "I'll see you later. If the Sandinistas are dancing, I'm going to dance too." So I danced. In the middle of the room, I heard a woman calling out, "Mrs. Bonpane!" I tried to figure out who could know me down here. It was Carolina, an ESL student who I had taught at Kennedy Adult School. She was one of the upper-class people and was definitely not pro-revolution, but was dancing with the Sandinistas. When we started talking, she said, "I'm getting out of here. I'm not staying too much longer. Everything is going to change now that they're in." In the meantime, she was still trying to enjoy herself.

We got to travel around the city. Already, they had renamed the streets. On Sunday, there was a big procession celebrating the vaccination of the local children. That whole area had never been vaccinated before. They made a major ceremony of it for all the kids who were getting vaccinated. It was like a Catholic ceremony. It was so amazing, what with all the literacy campaigns and everything.

By the time I got back home, I was on cloud nine. I felt rejuvenated, and I wasn't so mad at Blase anymore. In fact, I started doing speaking engagements the very next week.

I asked Colleen, who was about ten, whether she wanted to go with me to my speaking engagement about Nicaragua or with Blase, who was speaking elsewhere.

She said, "I don't want to go with either. I want to stay home. I don't want to go on any more demonstrations."

I think Colleen struggled with our activist lifestyle more than anyone, though I tried to be there for her as much as I could.

Shortly after my trip, Rosario asked us again if we would bring a delegation down to Nicaragua. She said she wanted us to bring the intellectuals. That became increasingly funny as the years went on. What she really wanted was celebrities, people who had big names in our country, to come down and come back to the US and talk about what they had seen. They were aware of the growth of the Contra movement from the start, and were trying to get ahead of it. She said, "We want them to go back and be our emissaries. Can you do that?" We said we could.

We were still operating out of our home in Mar Vista. Blase contacted Ed Asner, Martin Sheen, and Kris Kristofferson, who I believe was there but who may have come on a later delegation. Eventually, we also had Oliver Stone, Mike Farrell, and a lot of others go on this first delegation.

Blase and I were planning to go down together because it was our first "official delegation." All the meetings took place in our home; we discussed what we were going to do, how we would get there, what could happen. Our kids were listening to all of this. Blase Martin was eight years old. He asked, "Are you both going?"

"Yeah."

"Who is going to sing us a goodnight song or read us a story if neither of you is here?"

We knew what he was really saying. He could hear all the reports that there was still shooting going on. He was worried that if we both went, neither one of us would come back. We decided right then that we would never take delegations together. One of us would always stay home with the kids.

So Blase went down with the celebrities. Rosario loved celebrities. She was a kind of Jackie Kennedy type for a lot of people; very sophisticated, very refined. She had been a guerilla, but she could sometimes have uppity tendencies. She wanted the celebrities there. They all went down and committed to doing everything they could to spread the word. After all our delegations, we always had a follow-up meeting. What was everybody to do? Who was going to write to the newspaper? Who was going to contact the radio programs?

The work was fulfilling, but things were getting really bad on the ground. The massacres had started all over the place. Whenever we went down, we always took people to the Contra zone right up on the border. We thought that was the best way to show what was happening because that was where the *campesinos* were being killed left and right.

In my first two groups, when I was completely crazy, I took sixty people down. The thing was, the only delegation I had ever led was the one in Cuba, and that responsibility came to me by accident. Blase had never led one either. We had to create something from scratch. Rosario had never had a delegation before, so we were her model. She didn't know what it should look like. I took sixty people in 1983. I only planned to take thirty, but people just kept signing up. We had preliminary meetings to prepare them, but we didn't really vet the people we brought. We basically took anybody that looked sane and decent.

Most of them had political objectives. We knew that. We sensed, and we later found out for sure, that there were agents who came with us. The girlfriend of Bruce Herschensohn, a right-wing political commentator on TV who had worked in the Nixon and Reagan administrations, came on a delegation. She had no interest whatsoever in what was happening with the people, so we assumed she was there for Bruce.

A lot of interesting people came down with us on these trips. In the later years, the Nicaraguans started calling them the "sandalistas" because they came down in their sandals. The Nicaraguans were always clean and wore decent clothes. Some of our people were like, "I'm here with the revolution. I don't ever have to take a bath again."

Some of them were hippie counter-culture types, but some of them were sincerely in the movement as well. It was a little like it was in the sixties: the more holes you had in your blue jeans, the more of a revolutionary you were. Rosario told me I needed to talk to my people. I had to start telling them to bring clean clothes to at least be presentable.

Our days usually went like this: We woke up and had a cold shower. I always forgot to mention that there was only cold water. After breakfast, we'd go out into the mountainous areas and meet the *campesinos*. They would talk to us about what had been going on with Somoza and what was going on now. They had already recognized that the Contras were starting this whole thing over again. When we went up to the border areas to see the *campesinos*, the fighting had already started. We would go up there during the daytime and leave before dusk because the fighting would start as soon as it got dark. A couple of times the bus broke down and we weren't sure we were going to get out in time.

Leading the delegation was challenging. I wasn't quite prepared to manage sixty people. Rosario presented us with a schedule for each day. She had a precise idea of the kind of people and groups she wanted us to meet. It was like, first we'll go here, then meet the Mothers of the Martyrs there, then back over here to meet some legislative leaders, and so on. We also went to the US Embassy and said, "What the heck are you guys doing down here?"

We spent our days visiting Nicaraguan groups. Very often, at night, after everything else was over and we had done whatever we could, there was entertainment. It amazed me. This was what I tried to bring back. Back home, at all of our events, we just had speakers come and talk. People always said we didn't have time to sing or do anything else. I said, "I was in Nicaragua in the middle of the Contra War. We spent all day up on the border, and at night everyone just wanted to go out and dance. They had this thing about the joy of life. Even with everythng that was going on, they would stop and say, hey, I think we need a break for a couple of hours." I used to tell

Blase, "I go down there to dance." I danced more in Nicaragua than I ever danced here.

I challenged Rosario about some of her plans. She came up with all kinds of rules in addition to the schedule she created. I was responsible for the sixty people I had brought, and they would ask me about these rules, or tell me about other places they wanted to visit. I tried to bring this up with Rosario, but she didn't like that. She would say, "I can't take all these requests. Just give them to me on paper."

All those people had so many questions, and I was supposed to have answers to them all. I literally never had a moment's peace. I used to set up a little office in a toilet stall and open my briefcase with all my folders and notes. It was the only place I could get anything done. Even when I was in bed at night, somebody would usually come in with a question. Eventually, I told them to write the questions down. I took all the little slips of paper and went into my "office" to make a list for Rosario of all the things people wanted to do. People came to me with complaints, and I had to try to tell her how the group was feeling. It seemed like she put most of her effort into the celebrity groups, which I found a little frustrating.

The first two years I brought down sixty. After that, I was down to thirty-five, just one busload instead of two. I would teach them the Sandinista Hymn so that we could sing it when we got to the border. I told them on the bus what we would encounter when we got there.

In those first two years when we were still celebrity-tainted, we were treated like the princes of the land by Daniel and Rosario. After a while, when we started bringing in more and more regular people, we realized that their interest in our delegations was waning. But we were determined to bring other people too, not just celebrities, so that they could go home and write articles and organize and go to visit our legislators.

I took eighteen delegations, and Blase took at least three times that many. After the first one, we had a delegation going every month. I trained other people to be delegation leaders as well. A number of organizations started as a result of people who went with us. There was a group in Seattle, and a group in Colorado that is still going, and Technica for Nicaragua. A lot of our people, not necessarily celebrities, but ordinary, everyday people came back and started these organizations.

In 1983, when we were just starting to organize delegations, we opened the Office of the Americas. At that time, everything was happening in our house. People would just show up and say, "Let's talk about the revolution." With two little kids, I just couldn't get anything else done. I could feel that my boundaries were slowly being eroded.

We had meetings at our house, and people constantly showed up with goals and plans they wanted us to help them with. I was teaching four days and four nights a week, and the children were still so young. It was just too much. I taught four days a week and four nights a week. It just happened to be a filmmaker friend who had made *The War at Home*, who was kind of the straw that broke the camel's back. On one of my off mornings, I was in my bedroom stripping the bed and throwing laundry all over the place. I looked up and there was the filmmaker friend. "How's it going?" There was no line that was not crossed. There wasn't a minute when somebody wasn't here talking about the revolution, and I had a few other things to do. I told Blase that we had to get an office outside of our home.

Over the years, various friends had told us that we should at least be getting our expenses paid for all the work we were doing. We had been paying for everything ourselves out of our teaching salaries. A lot of our personal friends, all of whom were very political, were saying that we needed an organization, not only to pay expenses but to promote this work. It was clear that the trouble in Central America was not going to be over. We had to do more. Adam Freidson, whom I had worked with at Medical Aid to El Salvador, said, "Why don't you get a board of directors started and we'll find you an office?" Okay, sure, we thought. Let's start an organization.

We met at our home in Mar Vista with a group that included Adam, Nancy Hollander, Ruth Shy, who became our first director,

Carol Burke Fontaine, and Mike Fontaine. Somebody said, "What are we going to call this? Let's give it a name." We started throwing out names and somebody said, "What about the Office of the Americas?"

I said, "Isn't that a little pompous?"

Blase said, "I was going to say Office of the World." He was serious too.

We decided on the Office of the Americas. The next questions were: where do we go and how do we pay for it? We had been fundraising for other groups up until that time. I ran a lot of CISPES activities, and we did fundraising for Medical Aid for El Salvador. After we started the Office of the Americas, we began fundraising for ourselves, for our own organization. When we started, we didn't have any money or a location. We started calling churches.

I called St. Augustine's in Santa Monica. The Episcopal priest was a woman named Carlyle Gill. She said, "We just had a parish meeting and everybody felt we should do something about what is going on. We'd be so honored to have you here." This was great news, but we still had to pay rent.

One morning I got a call from Martin Sheen. He had just done a film about the nuns who were killed in El Salvador. They paid him $25,000 for the film, but he didn't want to keep the money from the movie based on the nuns' lives. He asked me, "Can you tell me five groups doing this work so I can give each one $5,000?"

I said, "CISPES, CARECEN, Medical Aid for El Salvador, *El Rescate*, and, well, us—we are thinking of starting our own group."

He said, "You've got your first $5,000."

With that donation, we opened a bank account, got a telephone, and got started at St. Augustine's. Three months later, we had our first event. Of course, we didn't have a computer or a database or anything. In those days, whenever you went to a restaurant, everybody carried a business card or wrote their address on a napkin. We kept all those little pieces of paper. Some of them were alphabetized and some were not. Right from day one I had a group of about ten volunteers, and the first thing we did was to put all those scraps of paper on index cards. That was our first mailing list.

Ruth Shy, who was hired as OOA director, had been an organizer in the Nestlé boycott. She was an excellent organizer. When we decided to have our first event three months later, we had all the names on index cards. We found someone to design our brochures, stationery, and invitations. We had to type up or handwrite all the envelopes. We were going to use St. Augustine's Church for the event, so anybody who came near the office just immediately got sucked into helping. That was when I met my dear friend, Lois Davis, who became our events coordinator. We built up a committee. We had so many volunteers all the way down the line. There were a hundred people involved in sending out the mailings or making phone calls. I loved working with volunteers. I told Lois to get some chips and salsa, put up some balloons, and we'd see how many people showed up. Much to our surprise, people arrived in droves. We couldn't believe that the place was so full. More than five hundred people attended our first event. Dave Clennan, Jay Levin, the founder of the *LA Weekly*, Ed Asner, and Martin Sheen were all there from the start.

We learned something from that first event that would help sustain the OOA and make it the organization it became. We had celebrity support right from the beginning. With people involved in the movement, we had built up our own credibility over the years. They knew how much we were helping all the other groups. But we were trying to reach people outside the movement by going to churches and Democratic clubs, and to have Martin Sheen's name on our literature meant a lot. None of our celebrity supporters were just actors or musicians; they were all people of integrity that other people respected as much for that as for their skills as entertainers. That combination made a lot of the people who didn't really know who we were begin to trust us.

It worked the same way with other celebrities. Somebody who knew Martin Sheen would meet us through that connection, and it was as if they said, "Well, I guess if Martin trusts them, I'll trust them." So, little by little, in addition to Martin and Ed Asner, who joined the OOA Board, Kris Kristofferson, Robert Foxworth, and Jackson Browne supported us. The next thing we knew, we had a big Rolodex of all these people. Other groups called on us to get celebrities for this speaking engagement or that event that they were doing. I think our ability to work with other organizations and count on celebrities at the same time was an important reason we lasted while other organizations didn't.

Blase, Martin Sheen, and Daniel Ellsburg in Nicaragua, 1984.

When we got the OOA started, I had no intention of giving up my teaching job. We still depended on my health plan and salary. I was elected board president, and we started to have our board meetings. Although I was the president of the board, I was determined that I wasn't going to be the one to run the office. Because I was the founder of OOA and the president of the board, I would give the direction, but I wasn't going to get involved in the nitty-gritty of administration. I had my teaching jobs. Ruth Shy was the one who was really going to run the office.

As we were planning our event that June, Ruth announced to us that she got a job in Michigan working on the Nescafé boycott. She wanted to be closer to her family. We were devastated, because at this point, she was the OOA in terms of administration. We immediately went on a search to find a replacement. I came in for the summer, when I wasn't teaching, as the interim director. By September, we had found another young woman to be the associate director. I continued teaching. We had a lot of board meetings to work out all the logistics, but she was overwhelmed by the job, and by April, she quit. She just walked out. She had something like a nervous breakdown, leaving us a note that said, "I just can't handle this. This is over my head." It was a horrible shock to us, especially the way she left us. We felt terrible. The board convened to see what we would do. Everyone asked if I'd consider being the administrative director. Since we had lost two directors already, I felt I had to step in and become the director; it seemed we weren't able to keep anybody else. I gave up teaching at Santa Monica College and started as director in 1986. When I started working full-time at the Office of the Americas, I went on salary.

It was shortly after we opened the office and held our first event that I took my first group down to Nicaragua. Though I took sixty people my first two years, after that we usually only took thirty-five, unless we were taking teenagers. I had an assistant, Joyce Fisk, who was with me on the trips with the teenagers. We had two busloads. One of us, Joyce or I, was supposed to stay on the bus with the teenagers, but she always wanted to sit next to me. I would have to make her get on the other bus. We had teenagers and adults as if they were two different delegations, but we all went to the same places.

The teenagers were my favorite delegation. They were so amazing. Everyone thought I was crazy to take teenagers to Nicaragua in the middle of the Contra War. Of course, some parents said, "What are you doing? I don't want my kids to go down there." But other parents thought it was great.

The kids were sixteen or seventeen, in their junior or senior years of high school. I was not their mother and I didn't want to be, but I had to have some rules about what we expected and what our purpose was. What about drinking and smoking? What was the rule, I asked myself, because some Nicaraguans around their age were going to be drinking and smoking. We had briefings before we went down about the protocols, good manners in another country, rules around drinking and smoking, and reminders about what we were there for. I told them I didn't want them doing things in Nicaragua their parents wouldn't let them do back home. Once we got over that, they were fantastic. None of them were ever really difficult. My daughter went on the first delegation with me, and my son went on the second one.

They were all so vulnerable, in a good way—open to what they saw in Nicaragua and the knowledge that our country was responsible for all the Contras and all the killings. We went to see the Mothers of the Martyrs, who would talk about how their husbands had gone into the fields one day and never came back because they had been decapitated. It was really heavy-duty stuff. The teenagers absorbed it, for the most part, in a very healthy way, seeing how different our lives were, how easy our lives were, and what we could do when we got back home. There was one kid whose parents were really politically committed. He wanted to be number one activist. He'd say, "We've got to do whatever the Sandinistas want us to do." One night, he came to me crying and said, "I can't take the pressure." It was too much for him to absorb. To a great extent, what they saw was helpful, but it was so real that once in a while it really got to some of them.

There's one picture from one of those trips that I really love. We always got a day off to do something relaxing, and one time, they took us to the lake to go swimming. All of a sudden, we looked over on the beach and there was a group of young people coming toward us. They were in the military, and they were the same age as our delegation. They had been up in the mountains fighting. They only had a couple of hours of rest before they had to go back up into the mountains. They all went to one part of the beach, dropped their uniforms, and went swimming in their underwear. In the picture, I'm out in the lake and our kids and the Nicaraguan kids are playing "king of the mountain" and knocking each other over. When they needed to say something more than "whoops," they yelled, "Theresa, how do you say this?" I was out in the water translating for them.

It was so touching to see the quick bond that they formed; they came from two different worlds: the world of the oppressors, and the world that was rife with suffering as a result. It was absolutely beautiful. They all came back up on the beach and everybody had a soda. Then, the Nicaraguan kids went over and put their uniforms on and went back up to the mountains. Our kids said, "Oh my God. We're the same age, and they're up there fighting." I could tell that this really resonated with them—they realized how unaffected by the horrible things our country does that they can be if they choose to look away. The Nicaraguan kids couldn't get away from it. I was very moved to see all of our kids realize how privileged we are. When we came back, they did a lot of good work. They asked me to speak at many of their schools so that we could bring other kids down.

While we were giving a lot of attention to Nicaragua, we also realized that El Salvador needed us. In March 1980, Archbishop Oscar Romero of San Salvador was killed by a death squad. In December, three Maryknoll sisters were killed. Stories of other atrocities were getting back to us from El Salvador all the time. We had helped organize CISPES, but we needed to do more.

In 1985, the Contadora Group, comprised of Mexico, Panama, Colombia, and Venezuela, was trying to negotiate a peace plan that would end President Reagan's Contra War. A group of Norwegian peace activists decided to organize the International Peace March through Panama, Costa Rica, Honduras, El Salvador, Guatemala, and Mexico to draw support for the Contadora peace proposal. Blase got a letter from the organizers who said they wanted a US representative to participate in the march. Somehow, everybody always got Blase's name. He communicated with them and felt it was a really good idea, and very necessary. We held an OOA fundraiser for the march.

The more Blase communicated with the march organizers, the more determined he was to go. He said, "I have to do it. This is imperative. We're losing lives down there, and we've got to go." He had already started telling people about it, and everybody was excited.

The more determined he was to go, the more determined I was that he not go. I was totally against it, but not for political reasons. I thought it was a wonderful thing for somebody to do, but I didn't want Blase to be the one to do it for many reasons. First, I was worried about his safety. It was the most tumultuous period ever in Central America. All the countries were in turmoil or at war by that time, every single one of the Central American countries. The goal of the march was to walk through all of Central America. It was danger unlimited.

In addition, he would be gone for six weeks. I would be here running the office and taking care of the kids by myself. I didn't want to be left with the burdens of both his work and mine, plus my concern for his wellbeing. I was adamantly against it. We had many, many arguments about that whole thing, and I was really, really angry with him. Even when he went, I was still very angry with him, because I didn't think it was fair to us. He felt it wouldn't be fair to the peace movement not to go.

On top of that, we were worried about security at home too. At the office, there was a malicious group that followed us everywhere. We called them "Nemesis." They came to our events, yelled at us, called us communists, and threatened us. They, or others like them, called the Office of the Americas on the phone. They said, "I want you to know that we're watching you," then hung up. Two minutes later, they called again. Sometimes they did it all day long. We called the police and asked them to track the calls.

Blase Martin's room was in the front of the house near where we had our answering machine. One day when he came home from school, somebody was on the answering machine saying, "Blase

Bonpane, I hope you go to Central America and never come back. I hope you'll be blown to smithereens down there." It was a horrible, ghoulish threat. Of course, my son's name is Blase too. He had just gotten into trouble at school for defending someone who had been threatened by a gang. He had been knocked over on his bike by the gang members and he came home and heard that message. Then we got a message in the mailbox which said, "Good luck down there, Mr. Bonpane. We're watching you, and we know you aren't going to be here." It was a very threatening note. I thought, "Blase isn't going to be here, and how can I stay here alone with two kids?" We called the police. We called Dennis Zane, the mayor of Santa Monica, who was a friend of ours. It was very unusual for us to have a friend in the establishment. The police came and walked through our house with us. They told us to put bars on the windows. They gave us a black box and said, "If someone is breaking in, press this button. We already have all your monitoring information. We'll be there in two minutes." The black box was next to our bedroom, so every time the kids walked out, it was right there to remind them that we were under constant threat. Later, Blase Martin told me how much that affected him. Every time he walked past that thing, he knew what it represented.

Blase Martin had started a paper route shortly before that, and I was afraid. He was going to go out delivering papers at five o'clock in the morning, and I said, "No, forget the paper route."

So Blase left for the peace march, without my blessing.

As soon as they took off, the very first country that they went to, they were bombarded. Their bus was hit with stones and everything. Almost every country they went through, they met incredible resistance from the other side. They also met some supporters along the way, but I think the people who hated them were the majority in all the countries. When they got to the Honduran border, they were met by the military. We have pictures of the military, with their big gas masks on and their bayonets and their guns, meeting the peace marchers.

We got the pictures and the stories. Many of the marchers were writing stories and sending them back, including Blase. He called us whenever he could get to a phone. I don't know if it was daily; it depended on where he was. He called into the media as well and sent in their stories. I don't remember that any of them published any of them. But the OOA published them.

The office became overwhelmingly busy. People were calling us constantly, either because they hated us or they loved us; "Thank you for doing this," or, "We hate you for doing this." We were dealing with these harassers all the time. It was just a really tough period.

Of course, Blase got back safely. He was exuberant and thought everything was wonderful, as he always did. In terms of the movement, it was a good thing that they went. Somebody had to go, and it was good that it was Blase. I still thought that it was unfair of him to go when it put such a huge burden on me and our family. I felt that we were in this relationship together, and the fact that our work lives and our family lives merged so much was all the more reason that we should compromise on some of these things.

After the march, the OOA worked to bring all of the Central American Solidarity organizations together. CISPES was definitely the biggest one, and there was also Medical Aid for El Salvador, and Central American Refugee Center, CARECEN. There was the Southern California Interfaith Task Force on Central America (SCITCA), and Witness for Peace, which was organized to oppose Reagan's support for the Contras.

SCITCA focused on religious groups, which they primarily worked with. CISPES was becoming more of a national organization. They eventually started taking delegations to El Salvador. Witness for Peace was going to Guatemala a lot, doing different kinds of things, but they weren't doing delegations at that time, so we were still the main delegation group. Everybody started chiseling out their own place, and we all cooperated.

There was a little of what I call "turfdom" among the groups, just silly, petty competition. If we were doing a demonstration or something, people would fight to have their name bigger on the banner, or for their banner to come first. I was really disappointed to see this developing, especially in light of the bigger issues we were fighting for.

Teenage Delegation to Nicaragua with Blase Martin, 1987

For example, Blase did a lot of speaking engagements for different groups, but when SCITCA was getting ready for an event and they were looking for speakers, they wouldn't even consider him. Somebody suggested, "What about Blase? That's something Blase certainly knows about." Mary Brent Wherli of SCITCA said, "No, this is only going to be for people of faith. We're a faith-based organization." They were always using the term "faith-based organization." When we started hearing that, we thought, "If we're not a faith-based organization, I'd like to know who is."

That said, I thought it was silly that sometimes the activists looked at SCITCA with some suspicion. It was sometimes said that, though they were doing a humanitarian thing, a generous thing, and a very nice and sometimes dangerous thing, they weren't really political enough; they didn't really know what they were ultimately working for. I didn't agree with that sentiment. The important thing was that the SCITCA people knew that the treatment of immigrants was wrong, they knew these people were threatened, and they knew they wanted to do something about it. How much more do you need? You don't have to be a Marxist scholar to come up with that.

The OOA didn't do anything directly with the SCITCA movement. I think there was a mutual feeling of togetherness and working toward the same general goal, but we had our own agendas and our own things to do. I think many people in the SCITCA movement might have felt that they didn't want the leftist label. They felt that it might be easier for them to do what they were doing if they didn't have too many people looking at them as if they were leftists, communists, and all the names that everybody else, including us, were being called.

The solidarity movement consisted largely of Anglo organizations and Salvadoran organizations. In the beginning, there was a Nicaraguan contingent of local people who started working with us. When we were still working a lot with CISPES, there were always a considerable number of Latinos working with us. But when we started the OOA, it was more white/Anglo. We have never been proud of that. I would have loved it to be different, for us to have had more Latinos in our ranks and in the leadership. But we knew we were doing what we could for the local Latino community, and they came to us whenever they needed to.

Despite the differences among the various organizations, we had a wonderful relationship with all the groups. We cooperated on demonstrations and events. We all pretty much brought our forces out to the same kinds of events.

In 1989, OOA got together with several of these groups to form the Wednesday Morning Coalition to protest what was happening in Central America. Every Wednesday morning the group went to Mass, then they went to the Federal Building. The goal was for some of them, maybe twenty-five or thirty, to chain themselves to the doors or just hold hands until the police came and told them to disperse. They refused to disperse and the police arrested them. Everybody watching cheered. The media was there to report on what had happened. After they were arrested, they had to go through all the processing and spend the day in jail. At night, we could go to the jail to pick up our jailbirds. That happened every Wednesday.

At the time, our son Blase Martin was in high school. He knew that every Wednesday morning, his father got arrested. The kids went to school, I went to work, and Blase went to Olvera Street to get arrested. I was at the office when Blase Martin called. He asked, "Where's Daddy?"

"It's Wednesday. He's in jail."

Things slowed down a lot in 1989. Chamorro was elected President in Nicaragua and that changed everything. We no longer took delegations down there. Blase went down on the last delegation. He was there on the night that Chamorro got elected. After that, there was a whole different focus down there. In 1990 the UN peace process began in El Salvador and led to the Peace Accords in 1992. Central America was getting its act together. A lot of good things were happening.

Looking back, Nicaragua, after all of the torture and all of the lives that were lost—fifty thousand during the Somoza period and a similar number during the Contra Wars—really made us sad in many ways. We were so glad when the Sandinistas came in with the literacy programs, medical care, and all the things we had wanted so badly. When Chamorro came in, a lot of those things ended. After the Chamorro presidency, Daniel Ortega came back into power and at first was presenting new works. This changed dramatically very soon after, and today has become an authoritarian government, much to my sadness. He compromised financially in a number of cases. I was, of course, very glad that people weren't being killed by the thousands, but I wasn't happy with a lot of Daniel's choices. Many of the Nicaraguan leaders stayed with us when they were in Los Angeles. When Ernesto Cardinale, the minister of culture, stayed with us, he also said he was very disappointed with Daniel. He thought they were going in the wrong direction. He considered Daniel a traitor to the revolution. Daniel's vice president broke off with him. But all in all, he was a lesser evil than Somoza. The Sandinistas did transform a lot of things in the country, like medical care and education. All the literacy programs were wonderful. The Sandinistas, despite their shortcomings, brought about a lot of good.

CHAPTER 8

Changes at the Office of the Americas, Local Involvement, and the Iraq Peace Movement

In 1989, the OOA was faced with a pressing issue. St. Augustine's asked us to find another location. We had been at St. Augustine's since 1983. At first, we had a wonderful relationship. Reverend Carlyle Gill, the minister who was there at the time, was a very progressive woman who was very helpful. We didn't have to pay to use the church for events, and they let us use the sanctuary and the downstairs auditorium when we had a large group. But, eventually, Reverend Gill left and the new pastor came in. At first, he told everybody, "They're so wonderful. We love having them there." For three or four years, I think he really did like having us there.

Our relationship with the church really started to change with the new influx of homeless people. When he was governor, Ronald Reagan had shut down the mental hospitals, promising that the patients would be better off if we sent them back out into the communities. All of a sudden, we started seeing mentally ill homeless people everywhere, not just on Skid Row, but on the streets in Santa Monica. Naturally, people often go to churches when they don't have anything to eat or any place to sleep. They started coming to St. Augustine's. The church turned them away. They told them, "We don't have anything. We can't help you."

The church offices, the priest's office, and the secretary's office were all downstairs. Crossroads had a grade school downstairs—mainly for rich kids, though there were scholarships too. The Office of the Americas was upstairs. Little by little, these homeless people began showing up at St. Augustine's looking for help, but the church couldn't be bothered to help them. Some stragglers meandered upstairs to us. Our whole team said, "Oh my God, we have to help these people."

At first, we had no idea how huge this would become. It was just a couple of people here and there. We just gave them a little money to get some food. One night, Blase and I bought a woman dinner and took her to a hotel. We told the hotel that we were paying so she could stay there. We kept finding people and trying to help them. The next thing we knew, it was like a deluge. The word had gotten out, and they started coming to the church asking for Father Blase and Sister Theresa. They thought that we were part of the church. People in our office began to say, "Sister Theresa is right over there," or "Father Blase is over there." We were doing what priests and nuns were supposed to be doing because the people downstairs weren't doing it.

We learned that St. Joseph's Center in Venice was doing a lot of work for the homeless. We worked out a little voucher system with them. We gave people a token and a map and told them what bus to take to get to St. Joseph's. They had the Bread and Roses Café, clothing for homeless people, counseling, and lots of other services. We became a liaison for them while we were working with Central America. We also worked with the Ocean Park Community Center, which providied support for the homeless.

The problem just got bigger. An elderly woman named Thelma used to come in all the time. She was out on the street with nothing at all. We bought her food and, after a while, we told her she could stay in the restroom. At least she would have a roof over her head. The custodian found out what we were doing and told the people at the church. He said to us, "I don't think they want these people around very much. They are afraid for all the kids downstairs."

And indeed, the church told us, "We can't really have the homeless around anymore because it scares a lot of the children." We were horrified. We thought, "This is how you treat the homeless just because of these rich kids, instead of telling the rich people, 'This is your responsibility as Christians, or whatever you call yourselves?'" We didn't say that, of course. We said, "What are we supposed to do?"

They told us they were going to erect huge gates around the entire perimeter of the front lawn so the homeless couldn't enter.

We were never told directly by the church that it was because of the homeless, but they said, "We really need the upstairs space. If you would find another place, it would be really helpful."

Just like that, we got thrown out.

Aris Anagnos had just opened the Los Angeles Peace Center. His goal was to provide rent-free office space for left-wing antiwar and social justice groups in the Los Angeles area. He had always been involved in Central America, and later served on the Board of the OOA. Aris offered us space, and we moved into the Peace Center.

In 1989, I was experiencing what I'd later discover was severe menopause. I thought I was just exhausted, getting burnt out, which was a reasonable assumption, all things considered. I was feeling a lot of pressure. I asked for an increase in my salary because I no longer had my teaching job, which meant I had no health benefits. Blase wasn't earning any other salary at that time either. The executive committee of the board considered my request and several members said, "We agree that you should have a higher salary and health benefits, but we just don't have enough money." I was really angry; I didn't feel like they were putting enough emphasis on workers' rights. All along, we had talked about the importance of workers' rights and decent health benefits, but here we were, unwilling to help two people who were working full-time.

I didn't know I was going through menopause, so everything felt insurmountable. I couldn't just sit down and figure everything out rationally. I was angry with everybody all the time. I cried and didn't know what was going on. I was upset with Joyce Fisk, who was a volunteer in the office every day and had become a member of the executive committee and a close friend, and several other board members who had turned down my request. I decided to resign from the OOA.

This meant that Blase, who was the director, would be left without an associate director. We had a very organized board that met regularly. I asked Joyce Fisk to be president. I was mad at her, but she was one of the most intelligent, hard-working, competent women I'd ever met. I taught her to be the board president. I had also been the volunteer coordinator, so I wrote job descriptions for all the volunteer positions so they would know what to do and so that our administrative assistant could handle it. I tried to prepare everyone before I left.

Some people were upset. They thought that this was the end of the Office of the Americas. To them, Blase was the main speaker, but I was in charge of the nuts and bolts of the organization. But we had set everything up to make sure that the OOA would continue.

Garret O'Connor, a therapist on the board, suggested I take a leave of absence instead of resigning, thinking I just needed a break. The board agreed, but when the leave of absence was over, I wasn't feeling any better.

By that time, I was mad at everybody, even Blase and Joyce. Blase and I were going to therapy. Nobody was doing what they were supposed to be doing, as far as I was concerned. I was sobbing over everything. So I was crazy—totally not myself. But no therapist or counselor was about to guess what my problems were. Even the therapist I was going to didn't realize. Everyone just thought I was overworked. And I was—that was the difference between me and Blase. Blase was able to relax while he worked. I'm not. When I'm working, it's work, work, work, and when I relax, I stop and am totally relaxed. I was often mad at Blase because he was going everywhere and we never seemed to have time to relax. Anyway, there were legitimate reasons why I'd crack up.

I was also going to a doctor at Kaiser. The doctor knew that there was something going on because I was always feeling so tired and out of control emotionally. No one could figure out why. Then I started getting pains in my bones, knees, and elbows. I told the doctor, "If I'm in the car and I just hit my knees on the car keys, it's a horrible pain. I can feel this cracking."

He said, "I hope you're not getting osteoporosis. You better get a test. Of course, you are taking your estrogen?"

I said, "No."

I had been going to this doctor for years and years and all he said was, "Oh, I thought you were taking estrogen all this time." Then he said, "Maybe that's related to the other problem." He started asking questions and we both hit upon it. I said, "Oh my God. This is menopause." We discussed the pros and cons of estrogen and I decided to start taking it.

I had stopped work in January 1989 and started taking estrogen around April. During that time, I truly felt my life was over. I felt I would never work again. I thought I couldn't go back to the Office. The only thing that kept me from divorcing Blase was that I didn't have any money or energy to start my own life. The only thing that kept our marriage together was my inability to take that step because I was too insecure. I had started trying to live as though Blase wasn't my husband anymore. I was mad at him a lot. Our kids, of course, saw this happening. Blase Martin, who was sixteen at the time, was the one I felt most secure talking about this with, but it was hard for him. I was acting crazy. I went for a little walk on the beach every day and came back completely exhausted. I'd go back home, read, take a nap, do work around the house. I truly thought my life was over. I had completely given up.

Within three months of taking estrogen, I was totally normal again.

I was back. I wanted to go back to work. I didn't think I could go back to the Office, because the former administrative assistant was now the associate director. It wasn't the same when I was gone. The newsletters didn't go out anymore and the delegations had stopped.

A lot of things had changed, but the Office was still in existence. So I started looking for a job again, handing out résumés.

I didn't want to go back into teaching. I wanted to go into an organization. Nothing turned up for a while. I thought I'd go around organizing people's homes and offices until an opportunity arose. I was desperate to do something. My anger with Blase dissipated. We had been going to therapy all the time, and we continued to go even after I started feeling a lot better.

Haskell Wexler, Theresa, Martin Sheen, and Blase, 1990.

I finally found out about a job with Voters to End the Arms Race (VEAR). I was hired in 1990. That was a really great breakthrough for me because it proved that I was still a capable person. It turned out to be a six-month job, even though it was only supposed to be a two-month job. I worked for VEAR from October to April as the outreach coordinator to get an initiative on the ballot to stop the arms race and to get all the peace organizations to support the initiative. I became the coordinator, period, running the whole project. It was an incredible and interesting job.

I still did not think I could ever rejoin the Office of the Americas, partly because I had left, and partly because the new associate director was in charge and it didn't seem right to take over again. Then a major donor, Susana Dinkin, gave $30,000 to the Office to do a meaningful project. Pat Krommer of the Humanitarian Law Project, Blase, and our associate director came up with an idea of bringing in a North American woman who had been jailed and tortured in El Salvador. They decided to spend the money on a tour for her. When Susana met her, she wasn't that impressed with her story. Susanna came to our house one night. She said, "I wish that money had been used to rehire you at the Office. In fact, that's what I'd like to do because the Office isn't the same."

That planted the seed in my head and I said, "That's true. I left the office because I was sick. I'm not anymore. Maybe the Office would invite me back."

I met with one of the board members a few times and asked whether it would good for me to come back. He said, "I think a lot of people want you back." When we talked to some other board members, they said, "Absolutely." In fact, they were thinking of resigning when I left because their roles were very much diminished when I was gone. Nobody was really organizing them in the same way. People were worried because the OOA only had three staff members, and the problem was always finances. Once I got enough interested board members, Blase wrote a letter to Haskell Wexler and Martin Sheen to ask whether I could come back. They said, "Of course." Haskell even wrote a beautiful letter saying, "Even if Theresa came back part-time, the way she works when she is here, she would be doing full-time work." They all said they wanted me back.

Blase announced to the associate director and another worker that I would be returning. He was doing a satellite radio program at the time, meaning every week, his tape had to go to different radio stations. He had hired our new worker for ten hours a week to organize that and do his delegation work. We had been friends as well. When Blase said I was coming back, the two of them were very upset about it. I really felt that they didn't want be back because they didn't want to reinstate any of the projects that had fallen by the wayside when they were in charge. They hadn't initiated any projects.

When the board said I could come back, I had to talk with the associate director about how we would work together. Before, she had been more or less the secretary. I had to acknowledge her new position and try to initiate things without looking like I was trampling all over her. I could tell she wasn't happy.

Blase Martin and Theresa at their demomstation protest against bombing, 1991.

The day I came back, she took her vacation, which I thought was a mean thing to do. I had been away because I was sick. It was the equivalent of somebody coming back from a nervous breakdown. I hadn't been myself and I didn't hide that from anyone. Instead of having some compassion, especially because we had both worked together before and were friends, she didn't want me to come back. Before I had left, on her birthdays, I would bring her flowers or have the board do something for her. I almost always threw a birthday party for her at my home and let her invite whomever she wanted. If she went on a vacation, I'd have flowers on her desk when she came back. When I came back, she had written "Welcome Back" on a little bitty Post-it note and left it on my desk. It was like a slap in the face. I was healthy again and I thought, "I have to clear out my head and figure out what is going to bother me and what isn't."

A bigger source of stress was that there was never enough money coming in, no matter what. After Nicaragua had fallen to Chamorro, interest in Central America had subsided. We hadn't been sending out our newsletter regularly anymore or holding any more house parties. A lot of things had stopped, and even though we were starting everything up again, it wasn't enough. There wasn't enough money for all the salaries, so we had a meeting to discuss all of us going on unemployment. At least that way, we'd be getting something, because there definitely wasn't enough to pay all of the salaries. There were four of us. It was still too much. Blase and I decided to go on unemployment because we wanted to keep the office running and still pay the bills. No one liked the idea of going on unemployment because, as low as their salary was, unemployment was even less. Our associate director said that they had to go and look for another job, so they let me fire them. Blase and I ended up on unemployment for the better part of two years.

While we were going through all of this, the Middle East had started heating up. Our work with the Middle East was very different from what we had done with Central America. For one thing, we didn't bring delegations. Blase went on a delegation to Iraq with

Amy Goodman and a lot of other people at Christmas in 1990. We knew the bombing was coming in January. We hoped that if a group of peacemakers went to Iraq at the very time that decisions were being made, maybe they would get enough world attention to stop it. Unfortunately, the delegation was not successful, although we made a dent.

The whole Peace Center was practically a combat zone. Every nook and cranny was being used. We had groups trying to figure out the Middle East Peace Coalition. We had a lot of newsletters that went out. Every single Saturday we had a demonstration in Westwood. People on the other side were harassing us, of course, calling us "communist," "commie," and all the usual stuff.

We used all of our resources—the radio program, the speaking engagements, our mailing list, and organized people to educate about Iraq and to plan demonstrations. We knew that the bombing was going to start on January 1991. Along with a number of other peace groups, we had all planned a big demonstration to try to prevent the bombing. We had it at the Federal Building, and a lot of us had decided to do civil disobedience so that we would get more media coverage and get more people's attention about it.

We had to go to classes for civil disobedience. My son Blase Martin went with us. Colleen was at UC Berkeley at the time. Blase, Blase Martin, and I went down to the Federal Building. The demonstrators separated into those who were not going to do CD and those who were. At that point, we just stayed there and the police came and arrested us. Then they pushed us down to the ground on our stomachs and handcuffed us from behind. Blase and I were lying together on the ground, handcuffed, when we heard Blase Martin fall onto the other side, saying, "Hi, Mom. Hi, Dad."

They took away all of our possessions. I had known that this was going to happen, of course. What I didn't know then was that I'm a diabetic. I thought I was just hypoglycemic at the time, so if I didn't have something to eat every couple of hours, I would start getting dizzy and sweaty and start to pass out. I knew I had to have something. I was more afraid of getting arrested for that reason than any other.

Theresa and Blase, 1993.

I had stashed some rice cakes into a little bitty purse that I had slung over my shoulder. When the policeman threw me down on the ground, it was kind of hidden. So I had my rice cakes, which saved me. The only thing I cared about in prison that day was to have my rice cakes.

They were horrible to everybody. They put us in large jail cells, one for women and one for men. There must have been at least sixty women, if not more. There were at least as many men in the cell next to ours. No water. Nothing. We had to stay in handcuffs all day with our hands behind our backs. Somehow I was able to get to my rice cakes, so I at least had that. There was a toilet in the corner with no wall around it. Everybody who had to go to the bathroom had to go in view of everyone else.

It was just disgusting, the way they treated us. One woman was feeling sick, so I called the guard over and said, "One of our women is sick. Can you have someone look at her or get her something?"

He said, "What's your name, anyway?"

I didn't know what that had to do with it. I said, "Theresa Bonpane."

He said, "Oh, Bonpane. You're here all the time anyway. What are we going to deal with you for?"

Actually, he meant Blase, not me.

At some point when we were waiting around, we heard yelling from the men's cell. Somebody had sneaked in a little radio and they announced, "The bombing has started. The bombing has started." It sent chills up my spine. In both cells, we all started singing "We Shall Overcome" and other peace songs. I remember thinking that this was the place I most wanted to be to get that kind of news. Later, my son and Blase said the same thing.

They processed us all day, put all our information in the computer, and ignored us the rest of the time. Then they let us out about seven o'clock that night. That was really the beginning of our involvement in Iraq and the Middle East.

After they released us, we helped to start a really strong antiwar movement. We were working with the National Lawyers Guild, Voices in the Wilderness, and several other groups. Some groups wanted to bring Israel and Palestine into the discussion while others wanted to focus on Iraq. There was a lot of infighting. It was kind of a turf battle. Blase and I thought that turfdom was dangerous, especially in solidarity work. So we started being peacemakers to the peace groups. We tried to organize demonstrations, but we were also trying to get the peace groups to come together. We constantly said, "Look, they're the enemy. We're not one another's enemy." This was difficult in the peace movement where so many people had these strong philosophical or political differences.

In a way, that lasted throughout the nineties, because after the bombing and the war started, we had the sanctions. We were always fighting against the sanctions, which killed millions of people.

Our work was different than it had been with Central America. It was heartfelt, but not in the same way. We both had a lot in common with Latin Americans. We had lived there and we were involved with Latin Americans here. It was like they were our family. With Iraq, it was all of a sudden, what are we doing over there? There wasn't the same familiarity.

At the end of April 1992, the police officers who had beaten Rodney King went to trial. The jury found them not guilty. Blase was teaching at the time. Freddy Schreiber, who was working at one of the other offices at the Peace Center, came over and told me the news. I was devastated. How much worse could things get? We had heard there were a lot of people from South Central who were going to demonstrate. Freddy and I, along with four or five other people from the Peace Center, went down to LAPD headquarters at Parker Center. There were a lot of people we knew. The demonstrators were mostly from South Central, so we were definitely the minority. We were there for a couple of hours. People were furious and frustrated. It was horrible. After a couple of hours, we decided to leave because we had done whatever we could, and we wanted to plan what we could do next.

On my way home. I heard on the news that the place I had just been, the very spot at Parker Center, had exploded five minutes after I left. People started turning over cars and setting them on fire. When I got home I turned on the TV news and saw that it really was the same place I had been just minutes before. Blase knew that I had gone to Parker Center. As he came home from school, he thought I was still there. It was very scary for him.

The next day when we came to work, a lot of places, even in West LA, were closed. Everyone was scared. Stores in LA were still being looted. We had a meeting to try to figure out what to do. Later, we were invited to South Central to do a cleanup, which is exactly what we did. On Sunday, we got our brooms and shovels and went down to help out. We went to a bunch of meetings after that with people saying, "We've got to pull the city together." That lasted a while. But nothing much came of it.

The *Los Angeles Times* recently ran an editorial that said a lot has changed. It said that the stores and buildings in the area had been rebuilt. That's true. A few more things have happened there, but nothing significant. Maybe there is one more of this kind of store here or there, but it's so minimal.

I recently heard an interview with the head of Rebuild Los Angeles (RLA). He said, "We've gotten five hundred million dollars in investments, and we've done a few other things." But the results all seemed so small. It's not entirely accurate to say nothing has changed, but it's inaccurate to say a lot has changed.

There are some groups in South Central that are still working to rebuild. A lot of groups did pull together, but there was some resentment towards the Westside. Some of the groups in South Central said that we didn't know what it was all about. They also didn't trust us to stick around to help when there wasn't a major crisis. There wasn't a feeling of real solidarity. We went to a lot of meetings, but nothing really cooked. It never went anyplace. I think that Crack the CIA Cocaine Coalition is pulling in more multitasking groups than others have, even though that's not their purpose. They have more of the African American, Latino, and white people together than the other groups have had. But their focus isn't South Central.

In the mid-nineties, I started doing more local work. After the Northridge Earthquake in 1994, I couldn't stand what was going on with the homeless. Nothing drives me crazier than seeing a homeless person on the street, especially in the richest country in the world. After the earthquake, when I was seeing all the devastation and even more people on the streets, I thought, "I've got to do something about this. I can't walk down the street without feeling terrible all the time."

Theresa at work, 1995.

I went to St. Joseph's and volunteered one morning a week where the homeless could come and shower. They could come and do their laundry and get case management and we'd give them a little bit of toothpaste and a toothbrush. It's just horrible, horrible that that was the best that we could do for them. But, it was good for me because it really made me appreciate, again, how much more we have than so many people, and how wrong that is. I worked with them for about five years.

I decided to help out at the Ocean Park Community Center one night a week as well. They had just developed a new place with a wonderful new program for the homeless. My job there was to sort out all the donations of clothes that came in. Everybody just dumped boxes and boxes of clothes. This was my forte, of course. They brought me into a room where they put all the donations and said, "Do you think you can help us with this? People come here when they're going to go out for a job interview and they need to wear something nice." There were some very nice clothes that were brought in, but the clothes were literally all over the floor. They were just strewn all over the place. You couldn't find anything in there. So I went to work on that. I did that for a couple of years, as well as my volunteer work at St. Joseph's. The *LA Times* did a cover story on this work.

In '95 I got a call from some people who wanted to work for a living wage in Santa Monica. They asked me to come to the founding meeting of what later became known as SMART (Santa Monicans Allied for Responsible Tourism). SMART was concerned that the many hotels in Santa Monica were not paying people enough money to live in the community. The tourists brought so much money to Santa Monica, the least they could do was fairly compensate the workers who catered to them.

I became very active with SMART and later on with the Los Angeles Alliance for a New Economy (LAANE). Those two groups were pretty much the same, but LAANE was doing more in LA and we were doing more in Santa Monica. I got Martin Sheen involved. He helped us a number of times. We got thrown out of the hotel with Martin one night. When the police came to throw us all out Martin went into his acting persona. He told the police, "I'm so glad you're here because there are things here you should be seeing." He turned the whole thing around and said, "Did you know that they're locking the workers in here and they're doing this and they're doing that?" The police admonished us and left us alone.

And we won. We won the living wage, but then a couple of years later the hotels took it away from us again. So we're still working on that.

Blase was doing more and more with Iraq, and I was doing a lot with that as well, but I was doing more work with Homies Unidos, The group, organized in El Salvador in 1996, reached out to youth in the Salvadorian communities in both El Salvador and the United States. Its goal is to end violence and to promote peace in the Central American communities through gang prevention, the promotion of human rights, and the empowerment of youth. I was asked to be on the board. I accepted the honor.

Family photo of Theresa, Colleen, Blase, and Blase Martin, 1996.

Iraq remained the biggest thing that we were doing at the Office of the Americas. Blase was also working with Haiti, Colombia, Cuba, and the Chiapas. He worked with a lot of groups, at least in a networking fashion. When they needed something, they would write and say, "Can you write a letter? Can you do this? Can you connect us with that?" My work was mainly to make sure all the programs got done, that the mailings went out, and that we got fliers out for the demonstrations. Our members were mostly people who had started out in the eighties with an interest in Central America and then followed us through to Iraq and everything else.

Blase and I had also joined in the Lori Berenson defense. Lori was an American human rights activist who had been arrested in Peru for collaborating with the Tupac Amaru Revolutionary Movement (MRTA) and sentenced to twenty years in prison. We found out about her when somebody connected Blase with Mark Berenson. Blase called him and he said, "I need help." It was really Blase who initiated our involvement with Lori and worked a lot with the Berenson family.

As we got more involved, they asked us to be on the Free Lori Berenson steering committee. Blase and I and a group of others went to Washington to see how we could work on getting her out of prison. For a while we had demonstrations in LA. We put out literature about her, and whenever we had any kind of an event, we would have a table for her. When her parents came out, we hosted them and made sure they got around to the media in as many places as possible.

Theresa participating in a union march, 1997.

The steering committee's idea was to find creative ways to get Lori out of prison. The demonstrations were one. Lobbying legislators was another. He visited Lori in prison in Peru.

Sometimes the Berensons came to Los Angeles and sometimes we went to Washington for steering committee meetings. My heart broke for her parents, but our plans and strategies started to diverge at a certain point.

Today, Lori is free.

CHAPTER 9

9/11 and Working for World Peace

The 9/11 attacks brought all of our focus back to the peace movement.

The night we heard about the bombing of the World Trade Center, I was watching the news with Colleen. It was horrible to see the devastation, all the brokenhearted, crying people, everybody asking how could this happen in our country. Everyone was breaking down, crying and sobbing. It was deeply sorrowful. Everyone was saying, "My God, they killed our people."

It was horrible. But I could't help but think about how we do the same thing every day to the people in Iraq and all over the world, and we didn't extend any of this compassion and sorrow to those tragedies. I said this to Colleen, and she looked at me and said, "Mom, I hope you don't say that to too many people."

It was true that if a person said anything like that, everyone responded with "You don't care about our country." It was very hard to say that we should have some compassion. The attacks had been terrible, but what about the people who were collateral damage in what we were doing?

I said, "No, they're not exclusive of one another at all. I just think we should have the same sympathy. These people have been bombed for ten years. I mean, as horrible as the attacks today were, they are nothing compared to what we are responsible for in Iraq. So I just wish that people would see that connection and realize that this is a result of it."

She definitely was still saying, "Okay, I understand. Don't say it out loud."

The next morning I got a call from Mary Brent Wehrli, who had organized SCITCA. She said, "Are we going to do anything about this?"

I said, "Absolutely. I was awake much of the night trying to think of what we should do. Why don't we have the meeting here at the Peace Center? I'll call Don White and a couple of other people we know right away."

"Great," she said.

So we had a meeting in the open space downstairs at the Peace Center on September 12. Don came, and Mary Brent, Lisa Smithline, who was our administrative assistant at the time, and me. Little by little, other people seemed to have decided that this was the place to come to figure out what we were going to do. People just started filtering in. They all said, "What are we going to do?"

We decided that we were going to have a vigil right away, an immediate response to September 11. We wanted to say that we have to have the same compassion for the people of Iraq, that we have to always make that connection. By Friday of that week, we had a closed meeting upstairs in the Office of the Americas, because some people we didn't feel comfortable including had joined the open meeting. We decided to have a vigil on the following Sunday.

Two artists, Sally Marr and Peter Dudar, who were at the meeting. designed a flag in for the vigil. It was a kind of rainbow flag with a peace sign where the stars would be. We got the vigil together at a park in downtown LA. I think we had about two or three hundred people. We had some speakers, and we had some music. We talked about what had happened and said, "We've got to do something about this before our government turns this into vengeance."

Of course, immediately after, the government was talking about bombing Afghanistan.

At our meeting to organize the vigil we said, "We have to call ourselves something." We decided to call ourselves the Coalition for World Peace. Don and Mary Brent didn't come to the second meeting, so I was the foundress of the Coalition for World Peace. People who wanted to join us started coming out of the woodwork. Within a week we had a website. People just got started. I never saw anything organized so amazingly quickly. People were determined to get our voice out there. About a week or so later, we had another big demonstration down by MacArthur Park and a couple hundred people that came to that, as well. We started having demonstrations all the time at that point.

One of our goals was to affiliate with other groups. Act Now to Stop War and End Racism (ANSWER) was one of the groups that started around that same time. They became one of the most powerful organizations in the country doing this work.

Jim Lafferty, who had his office at the Peace Center at the time, was very much a part of ANSWER while I was coordinating the Coalition for World Peace. We tried to work together, but it didn't really click. There were lots of differences between the organizations. As people started coming to the Coalition for World Peace, we realized that we wanted to use different strategies to try to get middle and upper-class people and establishment people, not just movement people. We wanted to go to churches and talk to people who didn't necessarily even consider themselves liberal, but were at least humanitarian. We wanted to make it safe for other people to come to demonstrations.

We split along strategic lines. We had the same basic goals, except that we really did want to reach out to people in a different way. At times, we had an uneasy relationship, but overall, we got over it and we were friends, even though we stayed apart as a group.

In our Coalition for World Peace outreach, we tried to get speakers out to churches and organizations. The Interfaith Communities United for Justice and Peace (ICUJP) was organized shortly after the Coalition, so we tried to merge with them. We had meetings with ICUJP and ANSWER, and some other group that was trying to get something started. We tried to get a coalition that would reach out to all the religious groups. . We wanted to go to high schools and colleges to try to get students.

Martin Sheen, Theresa, Blase, Lisa Smithline, Greg Palast, and Ronnie Kovic
at our annual Office of the Americas event, 2002.

ANSWER wanted United for Peace and Justice to join with them, but they diverged on one major issue: Palestine. Both groups realized that Israel and Palestine are, in many ways, at the center of all of these problems and that the Palestinians are the most oppressed group in the Middle East. There was general agreement that we had to put our emphasis on achieving Palestinian liberation. There was a lot of infighting. People were calling ANSWER communists, and even people in the movement thought ANSWER was going too far. Other groups felt that ANSWER focused too much on anti-imperialism. In the end, the Coalition for World Peace felt that our strategy would be more effective in reaching the people we wanted to reach.

I always thought ANSWER was doing some remarkable work with demonstrations. Many of the major demonstrations around Los Angeles were organized by ANSWER. So I have remained a strong supporter of ANSWER, even though I sometimes disagree with their rhetoric. I continued to work with them. We got the word about their activities out to our membership. Every week we sent out mailings with their information. I also have done some fundraising for them. I wrote a letter to some celebrities asking them if they would sign a letter going to other people in the movie industry asking for money for the mobilization. Some of them are big names. Several of them agreed. ANSWER really did much of the organizing and we just tried to bring in troops for them.

Theresa and Blase on the beach at the Santa Monica Pier, 2005.

I resigned from the Coalition for World Peace when I was diagnosed with diabetes. My endocrinologist said she didn't think I should be working at all. She told me, "You really should retire." I have diabetes, a hypothyroid condition, high blood pressure and cholesterol, and I have a cyst on my thyroid. She felt that my system was fighting so many things that I shouldn't be working. So I had to pull back to working only four hours a day instead of eight.

When I did that, I thought, "I've got to put all my time into staying at the Office of the Americas." So I resigned from the Coalition for World Peace. I still do what I can for them, but basically, I don't go to any of the organizations. The same is true with ANSWER. I told Jim, "You know what I can help with and what I'll do, so you go to the meetings and let me know what you need." I don't go to a lot of meetings like I used to.

OOA Event with Harry Belafonte and Gore Vidal, 2008.

Looking back on the peace movement I think it has changed over the years. I didn't get back from Chile until '67, so I wasn't part of the early peace movement in the sixties. From '67 on, I felt that within the peace movement, people had many unifying issues, like the draft, getting them involved. A lot of the counterculture movement was more about the kids themselves and their lifestyle than it was really about stopping the war.

I think that although there was a lot of goodwill and sacrifice during that time, in general, the peace movement is more mature now. Despite the fact that rifts between groups still exist, I think people are trying much harder to close those rifts.

The thing that we didn't have at that time was enough young people. Today, that has changed immensely.

Another celebrity-filled OOA event!

Unfortunately, we have had a hard time recruiting college-age kids. One of the solidarity activists, I forget who, said that during the sixties, we would have been glad to have someone with gray hair in the movement.

At that time, when we went to the colleges or high schools to talk to kids, they were so excited and motivated and said, "Right on," and, "Oh, God, this is fantastic. We're going to . . ." But it would die out very, very quickly. I think that they were sincere about it, but they weren't profoundly caught up in it. Maybe it was a lapse on our part as well, that we didn't know how to keep them motivated.

We worked really hard on that with the Recruiters for Peace program. We have tried to counter the military recruiters on campus. Volunteers choose a school that they will adopt to go to regularly and do counter-recruitment on the campus. The Coalition against Militarism in our Schools, founded by Arlene Inouye, originally developed this campaign. We've just engaged the OOA membership in the program that she's already begun.

Women's March with the Grandchildren, 2017.

Arlene, I think, is giving more leadership than we ever did to the youth in terms of keeping them active and engaged. She's out on the campuses all the time working with them.

As time went on, we always, always seemed to have new causes and always will. In April 2019, Blase passed on. His favorite quote from the Bible was, "Life is changed, not taken away," and his last words to me were, "I love you, always." I am sustained by these words and we continue to walk side by side. I could not have asked for a more wonderful partner, my children, and grandchildren, nor a more fulfilling life. I am sustained.

Epilogue

I'll close by answering a question I have been asked many times, "What is it that sustains you?"

I'm sustained by my history.

My parents were Irish immigrants who received only six years of education in Ireland. They were very religious and had strong moral convictions. While they were not political, they led kind, loving, responsible lives, and taught us by example to do the same. That still sustains me.

As a Maryknoll sister, I learned much about social justice and commitment that serves me to this day. My years in Chile were the beginning of my politicization, as I realized that no matter how much we did, the system was stacked against the poor. The changes had to come from justice, not charity.

After two years, I found Blase and he sustains me. Blase was beyond belief. Many people knew him as a dedicated activist, and he was, but you may not know he was full of joy and great humor. I really lucked out with that guy.

My children sustain me. Colleen and Blase Martin are gifts we never expected to have, and we are so grateful for that. They are both incredible examples of love, strength, adaptability, wisdom, and caring. Adaptability is one characteristic they have shown in so many ways to adapt to lives they shared with Blase and me. They did adapt, and they survived. They sustain me.

I am also sustained by our extended family. How very meaningful are our get-togethers during dinner, with a glass of wine, supporting each other through the joys and sorrows that are sprinkled through our lives.

And oh, our friends—what a wonderful enrichment from these wonderful, intelligent, dedicated, and humorous friends. Some of our friends are also workers at the Office of the Americas, and what a joy they are as they work hard, laugh harder, and organize, organize, organize.

I have been sustained by my colleagues in the peace movement and at the Peace Center. Every day at the Peace Center is filled with people who care so much about what is happening and who work so hard to make a better world.

Blase and Theresa, 2007.

When I look at the world, I think I have to do something. I could not live with myself if I hadn't done anything, even though much of what I've done has not produced tangible results. I haven't stopped this war or that other one, but I feel that I've led the kind of life that my conscience tells me to lead. It's been a very full life and a very rich life, not monetarily, but in other ways. A very happy life. I mean, what else would I do? Sit home and watch television? I don't have any intention of ever retiring. I think I may have to keep pulling back a little bit here and there, slowing down some, but that would be the most, I guess. I have some hope that I can still make some difference.

As I read the daily newspaper and feel we are probably in the worst period of American history, I refuse to lament, but instead try immediately to transform my grief and anger into energy to think about about how to use our efforts, websites, emails, listservs, telephones, house parties, etc., into changing the world's situation. I am sustained by being a part of the peace and justice movement.

One of my favorite expressions is, "*La lucha misma es la victoria.*" "The struggle itself is the victory." We have not seen many victories, but every time we stand up to injustice, war, and oppression, we are ahead of the game. We have not given in to despair or inaction, but instead, we struggle and fight for justice and peace. We are victorious.

Every week we hear that we don't have another penny for firefighters, teachers, or libraries. But we always have money when there are bombs to be sent. Our delegations have shown us that we are dealing with mothers who cry and children whose lives will never be the same. Many of the young people that we send off to war come back changed forever. We must have the will to stop war. When you see the tears and hear the stories of the mothers of the martyrs, you realize that there should be no more victims.

Another permanent part of our work which points the path to peace is the saying, "Don't mourn, organize." *Si se puede.*

All in all, a lot has been accomplished. Maybe the results weren't—and never will be—all that we want them to be. But what's the alternative?"

I decided long ago that my spirituality was not as a Catholic, but as a person who tries to make this world a better place. I really feel that if there is a God, I'm going to get along with him just fine.

Afterword

I did not write much about my children in the pages preceding this, as I believe my children will write their own stories if they choose to do so. For me, my life changed when, in 1970, I married Blase Bonpane. Never did either of us think we would have such a day. We could not have been happier. Then, later in 1970, Colleen was born, and two years later, Blase Martin.

Left to right: Blase Martin, Colleen, Ossian
Above: Blase

How amazing that after our long but meaningful interlude, we now have two children. Our lives were and are full of gratitude. Yes, we did it all—Lamaze birth, nursing, nursery co-op two days a week—to be with them and to learn more about parenting. Next came the YMCA Adventure Maidens, Adventure Guides, Blue-birds, Little League, YMCA trips, major differences. Our lives were challenged from day one, literally, and we grew together during those years.

Left to right: Gianna, Colleen, Chiara, Blase Jairo, John

Left to right: Nola, Jen, Ossian
Bottom: Blase Scott

Left to right: Blase Martin, Nola, Ossian
Bottom: Blase Scott

Left: Ossian, Blase Scott, Theresa, Blase Jairo, Chiara, Nola, Blase
Above: Gianna

There were many tumultuous experiences, and many lovely ones too. But I think that our very busy lives were, at times, difficult for our children. They are now amazing parents with their own children, three each! Blase Jairo, Chiara, and Gianna Londono, Colleen's family. Ossian, Nola, and Blase Scott Briar Bonpane, Blase Martin's family. Notice a few named Blase here and there!

Colleen is now an ob-gyn at Kaiser, and Blase Martin is teaching in the Humboldt School District. They live very fulfilled lives to say the least.

And now, my Blase, my spouse, is one of the kindest, most joyful human beings, one who gave joy to all who knew him. Blase played piano concerts for me many evenings, playing one song after another, folk, religious, political, romantic, you name it. Blase passed on in 2019 and is present to me always, to this day. I am a truly blessed and grateful person for all I have been given in this life of now eighty-eight years.

My cup runneth over.

Theresa

Biographical Note

Theresa Bonpane is a lifelong activist and peace advocate fighting for human rights and addressing the root causes of war and oppression. She served as a Maryknoll sister in Chile and became politically active while working with marginalized communities, realizing that the poor needed systemic change, not just charity. In the years since 1983 when the Office of the Americas was founded, she and her husband, Blase Bonpane, have collectively and individually received more than twenty-five peace and justice awards from many government figures, celebrities, and peace groups. Alongside Blase, her two children, and six grandchildren, she has been a leading voice in the peace movement and has spent decades working to promote peace, nonviolence, and diplomacy.

Printed in the USA
CPSIA information can be obtained
at www.ICGtesting.com
JSHW020916310823
47588JS00001B/1